Airport

Days and Nights,
Terminals and Runways

Front cover main image - Los Angeles Airport Theme Building (*Kevan James*)
Lower image - Heathrow Airport gate lounge Terminal 1 (*Kevan James*)
Back Cover - Korean Airlines Airbus A380 on final approach to London Heathrow (*Fay Johnson*)

Airport

Days and Nights Terminals and Runways

Kevan James, Fay Johnson, Tyler McDowell

With additional contributions by
Pablo Herrera

Opposite – One of the most admired and well-known images shot at Heathrow; Final approach to runway 27 Left *(Alexander Zur)*

'Can the magic of flight ever be carried by words? I think not.'

Michael Parfitt (Smithsonian Magazine, May 2000)

The sister volume to this edition is

Airport Days and Nights; Evolution

This book is published in the international English language market and uses the form of English native to the authors.

First published in the United Kingdom and the United States of America 2017

Copyright © Kevan James, Fay Johnson, Tyler McDowell 2017

ISBN-13: 978-1979983464

ISBN-10:1979983461

The right of Kevan James, Fay Johnson and Tyler McDowell to be identified jointly as the authors of this work has been asserted by them in accordance with the Copyright, Designs and Patents Act 1988.

All rights reserved. No part of this publication may be reproduced, stored in a retrieval system or transmitted in any form or by any means, electronic, mechanical, photocopying, recording or otherwise, without prior permission in writing from the Authors.

Contents

Preface 9
Acknowledgments 10
Overture 12

1 Trains and Planes 16
2 Blue Skies 20
3 Ground Ops 24
4 Wind and Fire 30
5 Stacked Decks 36
6 The Cabbie 40
7 UK Wings I 43
8 UK Wings II 55
9 Globetrotting 76
10 Conversation 98
11 UK Wings III 108
12 Who Shouts the Loudest 120
13 Flight 128

Helsinki, Finland *(Tyler McDowell)*

Departure
(Kevan James)

Preface

One can almost see the world, at least in the mind's eye, by reading about one place or another and how one reaches some of those far away and exotic parts of the globe. Perhaps, albeit somewhat loosely, Airport Days and Nights could almost fall into the travel guide category, with a fair bit of history thrown in - but this book, and its sister edition, are not spotting guides to airports or a history of them, although there is a significant amount of both included, particularly airports that have played a role in our lives and our journeys through them. It is a personal story – ours - and the written word often tends to reflect the opinions and experiences of the author, which, human nature being what it is, is a natural enough phenomenon of writing about them, as we have done here.

Most people have an interest in something, whether it's collecting traffic cones, stamps or travelling and seeing the world. It's their hobby, their passion, call it what you will. A few are lucky enough to have a job that allows them time (and the disposable income) to indulge themselves. Considerably fewer are lucky enough to have a job that allows them to do what they would actually do in their spare time.

Many people involved in aviation, from pilots, airline cabin crew, engineers, the bright-yellow jacketed figures working at parked aircraft seen from the terminal window, to the often harassed and hard-pressed check-in agents (those at least that have not been superseded by automation), work as they do because they like aviation. We are no exception. We also like taking photographs. But none of the three co-authors work directly in aviation (even though one of the three writes about it) but we are enthusiasts, and we have written and compiled the photographs in this book as enthusiasts. We like commercial aviation especially, which is why you can find us at an airport somewhere, taking photographs of whatever comes along. Occasionally we might get up at some peculiar time of the morning if we want to capture a specific aircraft or airline. We might even stay out late and into the night to do the same.

We make no claim, as authors, to have great expertise, neither do we claim be the most widely travelled. Indeed we have seen very little of the world compared to others but where we have been we have enjoyed. So we wrote and, for the most part at least, took the photographs in our books - not all, for we have had some help to complete the story and despite the limited nature of our travels, the amount of material means trying to cram it in to one volume would result in a massive (and expensive) book. So we've spread it out a little and put it into two books. We might even compile a third since the commercial aviation world never stops developing.

Hopefully there will be a multitude of people who will enjoy them, as much as we have enjoyed making them happen, making these books a real reminder of where we have been and where we want to go. We haven't written them in strictly correct terms so being honest, here and there we've played pretty fast and loose with our grammar but it is us. It is air travel from the passenger's point of view, the commercial aviation enthusiast's point of view. It is our personal portrayals and journeys through the air and, ultimately, our own histories.

These are our days and nights, our arrivals and departures at the terminals and on the runways of the Airport. Or at least, some of them…

Acknowledgments

Authors do not write books without help from somebody, somewhere at some time. The somebody varies from the parents who bought us our first camera and set us on our road to recording what we see when we see it to the husband/wife/partner and anybody with whom the author shares their life to the most obvious; those who make the subject of the author's writing possible to begin with.

A note must be made of those whose job it is to make air travel happen; the manufacturers of the aircraft we fly on, the airlines who acquire those aircraft, the pilots and crews who fly them and the engineers who maintain them; the air traffic controllers who guide millions safely through sometimes crowded skies and to the airports that we depart and arrive at and the people who make those airports safe, efficient and comfortable. Even when things go amiss (as they occasionally will) there is somebody working hard to put it right, often unknown, unseen and almost always unappreciated - there are thousands of airport staff everywhere and without them, nobody goes anywhere. But for you, we would not have anything to write about or take photographs of. Those airport authorities that gave us some additional support, not only in modern times but in years past; Heathrow Airport Ltd as well as its predecessor, the BAA, Tony Hallwood and Kayley Worsley at Leeds Bradford, Kate Lawson and Mark Luty at Guernsey, the media relations teams at Amsterdam Schipol, Birmingham, Cologne/Bonn, Düsseldorf, Frankfurt, Zurich, The Chicago Department of Aviation, The Los Angeles Department of Airports, the Port Authority of New York and New Jersey, Dallas/Fort Worth Airport, the Metropolitan Washington Airports Authority, the Minnesota Metropolitan Airports Commission, Sydney Airport and so many more. Airlines would not operate, airliners would not fly, and we would not travel without you.

Then there are those who preceded us - those who took photographs and wrote their own books, the books that made us think 'We could do that...'. The inspiration you provided gave impetus for us to follow in your footsteps and to those who have made their images available on Wikimedia Commons, you have our thanks for doing so.

A special debt of gratitude is owed to those who waded through our words and proof-read it all and put right our mistakes.

To all those who helped make these books happen, thank you.

The Authors,
Third rock from the Sun,
2016/2017.

Departing...
(Kevan James)

Overture

Travel makes you modest. You see what a tiny place you occupy in the world

Gustave Flaubert (1821-1880)

KJ

Begin at the beginning. We live our lives; we are born, breathe, grow, go to school, grow some more, work, retire, get older and ultimately pass on to somewhere else.

But here, during our mortal existence, there are constants; we still arrive in this world and before we find the next one, the time in between our arrival and departure can vary. Dramatically so for some, but we exist. We live our lives and find our passions. Like airports and aircraft. Many who share that passion mourn the passing of old aircraft at the eye-stretching sprawl of aircraft graveyards such as those at Victorville and Pinal Air Park in the United States, Kemble in the UK (there are others), where the stripped out hulks of once cherished airliners go to meet the scrap metal merchants axe - a tear may even be shed as a beautiful creation of humanity's imagination and vision is dismembered until it becomes merely shattered shards of aluminium.

Like ourselves, airliners are born, live, work and die. Unlike ourselves and our aircraft, the airport, once born, continues to grow. Occasionally some go the way of the old and are replaced by shiny, new (and usually much larger) versions, needed because the old ones became too small, too cramped and hemmed in by the growing community they were meant to serve - like everything else, once born, even a community grows. For the most part however, the airport never dies.

It just gets busier. Sometimes geographically larger but mostly just busier, and the busiest cram ever-increasing numbers of people into their terminals, which, of necessity and yet still within the constraints of the airport's physical self, must grow and become bigger to accommodate the numbers, numbers that inexorably and remorselessly continue to rise because of an ever-growing population.

But we are already a little ahead of ourselves. To find the beginning one needs to go back in time, to both legend and truth; Daedalus and his impetuous son Icarus; Leonardo da Vinci and his drawings of aerial machines. To the fertile breeding grounds of the early aviators, the Montgolfier brothers along with Pilatre de Rozier and the Marquis d'Arlandes, to Otto Lilienthal, Count Ferdinand von Zeppelin and Alberto Santos-Dumont. There were many more, some at the same time, yet even more later, like Antoine de Saint- Exupéry, Charles Lindbergh (otherwise known as 'Lucky Lindy') and R. J. Mitchell, all chasing, living and often dying for, the same dream; to soar aloft, to be as free as a bird and yet in control of one's movement through the air.

On 17 December 1903 the dream became real. Across the sandy dunes of Kill Devil Hill, near Kitty Hawk, North Carolina in the United States, Wilbur and Orville Wright flew. Controlled and powered man-made flight was born.

Time and progress are indelibly linked and others joined the increasingly large numbers flying; Alliott Verdon Roe and Charles Rolls in England, Voison, Cody, Farman and Louis Bleriot. Roe later became the founder of the Avro Aircraft Company and Rolls went on to partner Henry Royce to form Rolls-Royce, better known by some for building cars - yet still a long history of building aircraft engines. On 25 July 1909, Louis Bleriot became the first man to fly across the English Channel, taking thirty-seven minutes to reach Dover after departing from Sangatte on the French coast (how ironic the points of departure and arrival on a journey from France to England seem a century later) at 4.35am and winning a £1,000 prize from

Overture

the Daily Mail newspaper. Clubs and Societies were formed, air shows began to be held and flying went on, despite the hazards, or perhaps even because of them. There were new designs, new feats of aeronautical endeavour, futuristic imagination and a lot of crashes – since, at the time at least, it was mostly men who flew, it was mostly men who died for daring to dream of flight, Charles Rolls among them in 1910. Progress is still progress and the flying machine became marginally more reliable and, potentially at least, faster than more earthly means of getting from one place to another.

On 15 October, 1909, the German airline DELAG was founded, the world's first, intending to operate airships between German cities but also considering a link from Cologne to London. People were already paying for joy rides and from using any open and flat area, regular flying fields began to be established and still the early aviators held an unquenchable desire to aviate even more.

The human race has an unfortunate habit of taking a good idea, misusing and abusing it and noble though an intention may be, the dark side of human nature was somewhat brutally predicted by author H. G. Wells as early as 1908. In his book, *'War in the Air'*, he wrote;

> 'There is no place where a woman and her daughter can hide and be at peace. The war comes through the air, bombs drop in the night. Quiet people go out in the morning and see air fleets passing overhead – dripping death.'

Prophetic words…the military were quick to see the potential for use of aircraft, primarily to begin with as a means of reconnaissance and thus avoid their armies being out-manoeuvred on the ground. Even though civilian flying continued unabated conflict was coming and early aircraft were to play a pivotal role. In 1910, Eugene Ely, test pilot for the Curtiss Aeroplane Company in the USA, became the first man to take off from a ship, the USS Birmingham and the following January, he went one better and landed his aircraft on the USS Pennsylvania. In England, then Prime Minister Herbert Asquith, accompanied by Home Secretary Winston Churchill, were impressed by a Farman biplane being piloted by Claude Grahame-White, in a demonstration of bombing, using flour bags, and the delivery of messages as well as reconnaissance flying at Hendon airfield in north London.

On the cusp of war in January 1914, the world's first regular passenger service began, between St. Petersburg and Tampa in Florida, USA. Using a Benoist flying boat on the first flight, pilot Tony Jannus carried just one fare-paying customer between the two cities in twenty minutes.

Rather perversely, one of the benefits of war is the rapid advance in technology and World War One, as cataclysmic as it had been, did at least show that the aeroplane had a viable future and that societies across the world could be linked by it. In August 1919, the International Air Transport Association (IATA) was formed, air service agreements were signed and a structure for air services between countries began to emerge. Even so, it was the Royal Air Force (RAF) who began to link London with Paris on a regular basis, most of the traffic being of a military nature and the RAF also flew between London and Cologne, carrying mail for troops based in Germany. A little over a month after the first RAF flights began, on 25 August 1919, the first civilian flights commenced between London and Paris. Flown by Aircraft Transport and Travel (AT&T) the route remains to this day the oldest International air service in the world.

Airport Days and Nights Terminals and Runways

Around the globe, regular services were now beginning, often paid for by carrying mail and as time passed passengers. For most of the early years, it was only the wealthy who had the money to travel by air – decades would pass before airliners were to become reliable enough, safe enough and with enough range, to link all four corners of the world. But at the beginning, pioneers pioneered, innovators innovated, inventors invented and designers designed. Aviation was no longer the exclusive preserve of men either. Women like Amy Johnson and Amelia Earhart flew. Real Air Ports were built, airline companies formed and routes developed. Dutch airline KLM, today the oldest airline in the world still flying under it's original name; Britain's Imperial Airways, forging links to the country's colonial outposts around the world; Pan American World Airways stretched it's reach into South America, across the Pacific and then the Atlantic for the USA, Air France, SABENA of Belgium; by the end of the 1920s the great names of early commercial aviation were becoming established as the world's nations embraced air travel as the future of peace and goodwill. William Boeing built the Boeing 247 airliner, Henry Ford his TriMotor and Donald Douglas's DC3 became the last word in air transport sophistication (the DC prefix stood for 'Douglas Commercial', the moniker remaining into the jet age). Then almost everything came to a juddering halt in 1939.

Just over two decades after the last war came to an end, the world was once again scarred by global conflict - and again, as with the first, it brought about rapid advancements in aviation. This time around however, it was different. The aeroplane brought war to almost every civilian doorstep. Although some bombing raids had been staged in the first war, much of the fighting was either on the ground or at sea. But such was the remorseless march of invention, this time bombs fell in life-ending numbers and as H. G. Wells had predicted, there was no hiding place, for women, their daughters or their sons. Cities were flattened, infrastructure either severely damaged or destroyed.

The ultimate came in 1945 when a United States Boeing B29 Superfortress long-range bomber dropped the first atomic bomb on Japan, still today the only country ever to have suffered nuclear attack.

Wars are born, live, grow and die, just as with almost everything. They are finite – eventually fighting has to stop. Eventually. Sometimes the fight can last an interminably long time, sometimes it is mercifully short. However long its life may be, what armed dispute leaves behind (apart from destruction) can be remarkably beneficial. The airport was no longer a grass field, prone to causing flight cancellations if it was too wet and muddy; concrete runways had been laid to handle aircraft that were much bigger, heavier and had longer range than their pre-war counterparts. To get the world working again after 1945 meant getting air services working again. Pre-war agreements were ratified and rewritten, conventions and protocols agreed to allow air services to cross borders. For years those agreements limited the way in which air travel was run, a structure that saw national carriers operate routes, all subject to restrictions and conditions. But the afore-mentioned remorseless march of invention remains remorseless and always continues. Invented in Britain, Frank Whittle's jet engine, still a product of war, became the standard for civilian airliners and the aircraft themselves became larger, faster and then larger again (although with one notable exception, not much faster). Demand rose, fares tumbled, the constricting bars of the old order were taken down, a new era ushering in frequency, availability and affordability.

Ninety-seven years, almost a century after the formation of IATA, new aircraft replace old aircraft as technology improves to make them quieter, more fuel-efficient and with fewer emissions as aviation does its part to make the world cleaner. Air

Overture

travel continues to grow as demand continues to rise and airports continue to expand.

❑

1
Trains and Planes

All great achievements require time

Maya Angelou

KJ

It takes seven hours and thirty minutes to fly from London Heathrow to New York John F. Kennedy, or JFK as it is more often known. It can take a little less, occasionally more, depending on wind speed over the North Atlantic. Wind is the single most powerful force in aviation and can be the aircraft's greatest friend or on occasion, its worst enemy.

For the most part however, it's a friend but the prevailing wind direction between London and New York is towards Europe, meaning aircraft heading to the North American continent fly against it – into a headwind. So it takes seven hours and thirty minutes between LHR and JFK although on average, an hour less coming the other way - with the wind now pushing the aircraft along, the USA to Europe means sixty minutes less flying. Until 2003 one could do the westbound flight in half the time, eastbound even less, if one had the money to fly Concorde but the end of the supersonic airliner in November of that year meant it was, once again, seven hours and thirty minutes to reach New York from London, both for the wealthy in first class and for the more financially thoughtful in economy.

Even in the era of Concorde, of big new airport terminals and not so big old terminals, the always present problem for air travellers was and remains, getting to the airport to begin with. For most, it used to mean getting on the airport bus, or if one was a little more monetarily secure and could avoid being ripped off by the unscrupulous, a taxi ride. Either way means dealing with road traffic and often a lot of it. The problem has been, and still is at some airports, a hurdle to overcome and in New York probably one of the most infamous stretches of highway is the Van Wyck.

Leading south from La Guardia Airport (LGA) to JFK, with road users from Manhattan meeting it halfway along, the Van Wyck Expressway is well known for its heavy use, as is the smog that hangs over Los Angeles, driven by the love affair between Americans and their cars - a throwback perhaps to the days of old when to get anywhere one needed a horse, and the independence of movement threatened by horse theft is why such a crime was so severely dealt with. In Europe, such a close relationship between man and beast, in terms of personal transport at least, has never been so entrenched and Europe has led the way in easing the passage of the airline traveller between city and airport with the use of the train.

The glory days of rail travel may well be in the past, although there are many who will disagree, but the train, even for lengthy enough distances overland, was supposed to be replaced by the plane. The train however, has made and is making, something of a comeback. As long ago as 1977, the London Underground, or the Tube as it is usually known, opened an extension to Heathrow, thus relieving some of the congestion on the M4 motorway and through LHR's tunnel and bringing much of London and beyond within direct reach of train travel. More recently the Heathrow Express offers a fifteen-minute ride from London's Paddington Station to the airport. Around the world, rail links from city centres have been or are becoming the norm. Even between cities themselves, fast train services have, to one degree or another either replaced air services or at least supplemented them to the point where flights can be reduced significantly.

What might seem a little strange is the idea of taking a train to catch a plane is not new. Invented in Britain, the country took to the train with boundless enthusiasm

Trains and Planes

and in 1938, Gatwick Airport, then a grass field, opened a new terminal. Tiny compared to today's architectural statements (and to the building that succeeded it), it was nevertheless for its time advanced and futuristic. Circular in shape it was known as the Beehive, and aircraft were parked around it, linked to the building itself by telescoping covered walkways that were extended across the apron to reach as close as possible to the aircraft door, thus keeping passengers protected from inclement weather. The terminal itself was reached by a tunnel from the London to Brighton railway line and had it's own station, its signage proudly pronouncing 'Gatwick Airport'. The future was already present, at least in the County of Sussex, south of the capital. When the airport was rebuilt and reopened in 1958, the new terminal, known today as the South Terminal and located further north, still had a railway station linked directly to and as part of, the brand spanking new building. Both terminal and station still exist today, albeit in a much expanded form and both are busy, the railway station especially so. Even the Beehive still stands, a little way further down the railway line to the South Terminal, although for how long is another matter since the airport's historic terminal will be flattened if Gatwick builds a new runway at any time in the future.

Today, the airport train station has become a normal feature of the advanced terminal and at some the inter-terminal train is the easiest way to connect with flights. The rise of the 'hub' airport has meant large numbers of flights arriving within a very short period of time and then departing again not too long afterwards, with passengers rushing from one terminal to another, a feature most noticeable in the USA at airports like Dallas/Fort Worth (DFW) and Atlanta (ATL). The North Texas airport, geographically speaking, is one of the largest airports in the world, spreading its way across a mind-boggling 18,000 acres of land. DFW has five terminals with room for *another* five when the demand arises. Each are linked by computer-controlled driverless trains, a slightly eerie experience even today but the system works well and is found elsewhere, notably where it all began, at Gatwick - the South Terminal has its circular satellite and a similarly driverless train takes passengers from main building to gates in moments, as well as linking both the airport's terminals. At Birmingham, also in the UK, its railway station has a similar system connecting the train to terminal, opened in 1984, and both UK airports are now in to the second generation of driverless terminal trains, as is Dallas/Fort Worth.

There are numerous other examples around the world and London once again features, although not so much at Heathrow. The easiest way of getting between terminals is to use the tube but on the other side of London, City Airport is easily reached via the Docklands Light Railway (DLR). Trains are usually without a driver, the system being controlled by a computer although from time to time an operator can be found sitting at the front keeping a mindful eye on things. When there isn't one, the same slightly disconcerting feeling of driver-free movement arises when travelling from the centre of London to City Airport.

Road access will never be entirely replaced (although one shouldn't necessarily rule it out), hence the huge multi-storey car parks to be found at most airport terminals, but there is something appropriate that the country that invented the train, the country that gave the world the jet engine and the country that, to a significant degree, has been at the forefront of aviation development, is still leading the way in utilising a train to catch a plane.

The increasing use of trains to catch planes has seen many airports build rail links where once there were none. Among them are Zurich, upper left.
(Flughafen Zurich AG)
Centre, London Heathrow
(Kevan James)
and more recently, Denver, lower left
(courtesy of Denver International Airport)

With terminal redevelopments taking place right around the world, if not including them to start with (often due to cost considerations) many new terminals, as well as rebuilt existing facilities, will have the basic elements included in the design so that a rail link can be added as soon as funding allows.

In December 1977, the London Underground opened an extension of the Piccadilly Line to Hatton Cross, then reaching into the airport itself, serving Terminals 1,2 and 3. The line now goes as far as Terminals 4 and 5.
Upper left - T5, journey's end and downtime for the driver.
Second left - Terminal 4's station.
Third left - Hatton Cross Bus and Underground Station, with the building itself on the far left.
(all images Kevan James)
Lower left - despite the improvements to public transport worldwide, use of the car to reach airports is unlikely to end anytime soon...approaching Terminal 5.
(image: Kevan James, car: David Winyard)

2
Blue Skies

I don't make jokes. I just watch the government and report the facts

Will Rogers

KJ

The sky is never as empty as it seems. Other than those who live close enough to an airport to be aware of its existence, most people spend little time looking up, unless it's a momentary glance, a happenchance, a brief look that brings into view the vapour trail left by an aircraft passing high above, apparently making its way, unhindered and unrestricted, to wherever it may be going, controlled only by its pilots with no signs saying 'stop', or 'left turn only'.

The absence of aerial signposts doesn't mean there aren't any rules. There are, and the sky is as tightly regulated as are the roads, even more so if the truth be told. There may be no traffic lights, no pedestrian crossings but there are still highways in the sky to follow, instructions from air traffic controllers to listen to and places known as 'waypoints' at which pilots have to report their position. Waypoints can have some evocative names but are nothing more than a position on a navigation map, but they are still important. The system of air corridors and the rules that govern them are universal, found the world over and has evolved over the decades since air transport began, along with Bilateral Air Treaties, allowing airlines to operate services between countries and today air travel is the safest way of getting anywhere.

The rules and regulations governing air travel go back to aviation's early days, with conventions, protocols and the five freedoms of the air; the freedom to fly over a country without landing; the freedom to make a 'technical' landing to refuel or undertake repairs; the right to fly from one's own country to another; the right to fly from another country to one's own; and the right to fly between two foreign countries on a service that ends or begins in one's own country.

Most airline traffic falls under third or fourth freedom rights, which is that between two countries carried by the airlines of those two countries. Fifth Freedom rights are a little different, allowing, as one example, Air India to sell tickets to and carry passengers between London Heathrow and New York and in the opposite direction as well as between India and the UK. There are others, like Garuda Indonesia Airlines between London and Amsterdam, in direct competition with British Airways and KLM.

Today, there are numerous airlines, headquartered in one country but with routes from, to and within other countries, one obvious example being Irish carrier Ryanair, who base aircraft around Europe and fly dozens of services to and from countries outside Ireland, although within the European Union. Hungarian airline Wizzair is another, with European Union liberalization rules bringing an end to the cosy monopolies once enjoyed by national carriers (usually state-owned) between cities around the world. Most air services, especially long haul, still tend to be operated by the major airlines of the countries concerned, like British Airways and Virgin Atlantic, the USA's American Airlines, Delta and United, all three of whom have swallowed up their competitors in more recent times. Most countries still have a 'National Airline' although many are now privately owned as opposed being owned by their governments and there have been a number of high profile closures, long-established airlines that were once the bastion of long haul (and in some cases short haul) air travel; Swissair, once one of the most respected aviation brands; Varig, from Brazil, Belgium's Sabena and Italian airline Alitalia – the latest formerly nationally-owned airline to enter bankruptcy.

US airlines have always been the preserve of private ownership and two of the biggest names to be consigned into history were Pan American World Airways (Pan Am) and Trans World Airlines (TWA). The two airlines held almost the sole rights to overseas traffic from the USA, Northwest being the third, primarily to Japan, competing only with the national carriers of other countries on services to and from the US. Pan Am went bankrupt, shutting down entirely in 1991 and TWA disappeared just a few years later, being taken over by American Airlines, Northwest subsequently merging with Delta.

The big change began in 1978. That was the year when President Jimmy Carter signed in to law the US Airline Deregulation Act and almost overnight, what had been a well-ordered structure around air travel in the United States became a free-for-all, with any airline allowed to fly any route and charging any fare. Hundreds of new airlines started up and hundreds of new airlines failed, beaten by the financial and route strengths of the legacy carriers, like American, Delta, Eastern and United. All four were at the time primarily domestic carriers, although with some routes to central and south America, the principal overseas routes being flown by Pan Am, TWA and Northwest. Europe was slower to embrace the change but demand was rising and people wanted to fly and fly cheap. The European Union (EU) looked across the Atlantic and saw that the American dream could be a Euro dream and as rules were relaxed, within the EU at least, any airline could fly any route and charge any fare - just like they could in America.

But any airline couldn't. Bogged down by the old ways of doing things, the big airlines, with big cost structures to go with them, found that adapting to a liberalized and low-fare structure was at best, fraught with difficulty, at worst, almost impossible. Only four years before US deregulation, in 1973, the oil-producing countries in the Middle East increased the price of oil by 70 per cent, sending shockwaves around the world with financially catastrophic results for commercial aviation. Fares went up steeply to cover the unheard-of increase in fuel costs, people stopped flying in the high numbers that they had been and profits became a rare feature in airline bank accounts. Some had still not paid in full for fleets of 707s and DC8s which were rapidly disappearing from the primary routes as airlines entered what a supposed to be a new era where humongous numbers of people would fill the new giants.

In 1970 the Boeing 747 had revolutionised air travel but empty 747s flying long haul routes cost serious money. Smaller short-haul aircraft and the routes they were used on weren't so badly hit but the higher costs of long haul and operating not just the 747 but also the new Douglas DC10 and Lockheed TriStar put most established airlines in big trouble, with some never fully recovering from the never-ending flow of red ink on their balance sheets.

Governments for a time propped up their ailing state carriers with subsidies but as the new compete-or-fail methods began to have an effect, the cost to taxpayers became too high a burden and when big business goes out of business, the results can be devastating. As Swissair found out, as Sabena also found out, national devastation is also national embarrassment. What made the two bankruptcies so interesting was the status of both airlines; Sabena were a typical, big, state entity, with a big sense of entitlement and big losses. Swissair were owned privately, despite the airline being the country's flag carrier. New EU rules were bringing an end to taxpayer-funded subsidy but Switzerland weren't in the EU. To fly across Europe however, meant the Swiss carrier had to follow the same rules as everybody else. The two carriers also had partnerships in various areas (in the 1970s both were members of the KSSU Group of airlines, the other two being Dutch carrier KLM and French airline UTA, the forerunner of today's airline alliance groups). Economic reality set in and the two carriers failed.

Other airlines had to adapt and the most successful are still going today, airlines like British Airways (BA), Germany's national airline Lufthansa, KLM and Air France, although the French carrier has had it's moments, being one of the last to embrace change but the airline is today stronger for its past troubles and is one half of the joint KLM/Air France Group.

The growth of the alliances between airlines, Star, Oneworld and Skyteam, mean today's air traveller can use seamless linkage to cross the world, although it can also be extraordinarily confusing to the unwary, who may book a flight with British Airways yet find themselves using a flight with a code from a different airline, using an aircraft from yet a third airline. The alliance competition comes from airlines like Ryanair and easyJet, amongst others, whose level of service to individual passengers has sometimes been questioned but offer the cheapest fares. Except...except...even the legacy carriers can now offer fares that are at least close to the low-fare airlines and in some cases even lower, using the internet and booking online.

Over recent years the industry has settled somewhat, the wild frenzy of the 1980s and 1990s having given way to a more sustainable methodology.

Airlines have come and gone and others will do the same but air travel was once a means of getting from one place to another used by only the wealthy. Today, it is within reach of almost everybody and everybody can and does, fly.

∎

Short Haul Low Fare

With the rise of low-fare airlines like Vueling, above, and Germanwings, main image, both of whom operate from Heathrow, legacy carriers have had to adapt their short haul routes a similar model in order to stay competitive, including British Airways *(Kevan James)*

3
Ground Ops

The purpose of life is a life of purpose

Athena Orchard

KJ

At one time, airlines employed their own ground crews to service aircraft in between flights. At major home bases, some of the bigger airlines still do. Airlines based elsewhere but flying to large hubs will often sub-contract ground operations to the larger carrier based at the airport they fly to, which is why you can see one carrier's aircraft being looked after by what is otherwise a rival airline. Even the biggest airlines will sub-contract their flights ground servicing to independent handling companies away from their home airports but in days gone by, almost all airlines took care of their own ground service operations. The need to cut costs saw many of those in-house ground handling crews disappear, even for some of the big airlines and out-sourced companies began life, looking to gain, and keep, contracts for ground handling. In the US, it led to the rather unkind sobriquet 'ramp rats' being applied to many of the new workers brought in to service aircraft in between flights.

There are a multitude of vehicles surrounding an airliner on the ground, from the most obvious scissor-jack lifters loading and unloading the baggage and cargo pallets, water vehicles to renew the supply carried onboard, fuel transfer vehicles which sit under the wing, pumping fuel from the underground pipelines found at most major airports although there are still plenty of fuel tankers to be found at some airports around the world, catering trucks, vehicles of almost every shade and hue, along with the ubiquitous honeycart.

Despite the breezy name the honeycart has a rather more mundane use; it empties the aircraft toilets. Contrary to a sometimes popular misconception, flushing a toilet in-flight does not open a small hatch somewhere on the aircraft's underside, sending the contents on to the unsuspecting population below. That said, it has been known for frozen chunks of blue-tinted something to make an unexpected arrival in people's back gardens. The blue colour comes from the liquid used to flush an aircraft toilet which can leak although the actual toilet contents don't. If it does, the liquid will freeze at the heights airliners fly, and being quite heavy, will drop quicker than it can return to its liquid state, hence the frozen monoliths that have been known to punch a hole in the roof of a house when they get to ground level. Those leaks that do become fluid once more have a record for leaving those on the ground wondering why they are getting wet when there isn't a cloud in the sky.

A honeycart is a long, low-slung vehicle whose operator plugs a pipe into the appropriate place on the aircraft and removes the waste, taking it away somewhere. I don't know where. I don't really want to know but it does seem to be something of a bizarre occupation. One can almost (only almost) imagine such an operator arriving home after work - 'Hey everybody, I'm home! I had a great day emptying the lavs today…'

Passengers have also been known to lose things down aircraft lavatories – meaning somebody has to search through the tanks of a full honey cart to find it.

Life gets more exciting with each passing day…

For the most part a memory from days gone by is the 'Follow Me' van, usually a bright yellow and black van with flashing lights and a sign on the roof facing backwards with the words, 'Follow Me' brightly lit. The vans would pull up on a taxiway near the landing aircraft as it touched down on the adjacent runway and the pilots would then do as instructed by the driver and follow it to its parking area.

Ground Ops

Once at the right place, the van would decant somebody waving what looked like a pair of table tennis bats, signalling to the pilot to turn, straighten up and then stop. Today, although the bat waver can still be found, even at the biggest airports, for the most part, pilots are given directions by ground radar, radio and their own up-to-date airfield and apron maps. For the most part it usually works but occasionally, especially at airports they do not usually fly into, it's not unknown for aircraft to get lost and spend time taxiing around until either getting clear directions or rescue from a Follow Me van. Even old technology can still be useful.

One of the more obvious aspects to ground ops, although rarely thought of by the average passenger, is the means of aircraft leaving the terminal. In days of old, aircraft would land, taxi to the terminal, turn sideways and stop, usually with the left side of the airliner facing the terminal. The reason for that is almost from its earliest days, it was recognized that passengers needed to be separated from the rest of the hustle and bustle of servicing an aircraft so ground operations happened on the right side, getting on or off was, and remains today, from the left. With bigger aircraft and ever-growing numbers, 'nose-in' parking became the norm and since airliners don't have a reverse gear (with some notable exceptions – see later) a ground vehicle became needed to push the aircraft away from the terminal and to its taxi position, which is why almost every flight starts today by going backwards.

Known imaginatively as tugs, the early examples were simply any vehicle that had the power needed to push, or pull, an airliner. Even farm tractors were capable of doing so, the big rear wheels giving enough grip to do the job. As aircraft got bigger and heavier, specialist tugs became standard, both for pushback and towing airliners around an airport. For many years, the tug used a towbar, usually painted bright yellow, which attached from one end of the tug to the aircraft nose wheel, and some care was needed when pushing back and then turning the aircraft to face the right way. At some of the busiest airports, especially in the USA, with taxi space becoming limited, the contortions required could place a severe strain on the towbar and without the right training and practice, tug drivers have been known to snap the bar, something of an embarrassing incident for all concerned.

This may sound obvious but its worth saying anyway - all airliners, right after landing, need to slow from flying speed to a safe taxi speed within a safe distance on the runway, whatever the weather. The loud roar of reverse thrust from the engines, which even today can worry less frequent and occasional flyers, is the standard means of slowing down. Airliner engines are remarkably powerful and there is a perfect logic to using the power available on take off in the opposite direction to slow down once on the runway at the other end of the flight. Just so the uninitiated are aware of it, airliners do have brakes and they are used once the aircraft has slowed down, and of course, to actually stop. Brakes however, can get extraordinarily hot so use on a runway after landing is very sparing – wheel fires have been known to occur when brakes are used heavily so reverse thrust is the usual means of slowing after landing. That same engine power can and has been used to send an airliner backwards from a terminal, so taking away the need for a tug.

For a while in the USA, the Douglas DC9 and Boeing 727 aircraft used the technique, but it proved to be more problematic than anticipated. Firstly, when an airliner sits on the ground for any period of time, 'flat-spots' develop in the main gear tires, from the weight of the aircraft itself sitting motionless on the ground. Getting the aircraft moving backwards away from the terminal rarely proved an issue for a tug but under its own power more so, to the point where on occasion, the pilot would have to move the aircraft forward a few feet (and thus closer to the terminal) to get the aircraft off the flat-spots before engaging reverse thrust to move it backwards.

I have seen it done – Northwest were one of the airlines to use the technique and I watched a DC9 at Dallas/Ft. Worth duly start its engines, doors closed and jetway withdrawn, and the reverse thrust buckets at the rear of the engines opened up and one could hear the noise as the power was applied. The DC9 stubbornly refused to move. Power off and buckets closed; then the pilot applied a little power and moved his aircraft forward a little, stopped, re-engaged reverse thrust and the DC9 gently moved backwards.

I made a point of asking what the forwards-then-backwards part was all about and the reply was, 'flat-spots...' There may have been more to it but that was the reply. The second problem was that with both the DC9 and 727 having engines mounted at the rear of the aircraft, they were tail-heavy and great care was needed when using the brakes to avoid the airliner tipping back on to its tail – and yes it did happen, thankfully rare but more than once.

The third issue was the increased fuel cost. Engines are not normally started until after the tug has completed pushback so any cost saving by not using a tug was quickly negated.

Today, towbars are still commonly found but at the biggest and busiest airports, tugs are very different. Available in various sizes and power, the modern day tug slides under the nose wheel and effectively becomes part of the nose gear itself, thus removing the need for a towbar, and moving even the giant Airbus A380 is more practical, efficient and safe. There are even, for smaller aircraft, remote control tugs and the latest developments enable the pilots to control the tug and thus their ground movements without starting the aircraft engines, so saving fuel and reducing emissions.

Despite the efficiency of today's ground towing operations, there was always something evocative about watching somebody using a pair of table-tennis bats to guide an airliner.

GroundOps

Above and left - the traditional bat waver can still be found, as can the 'follow-me' van.
Left - de-icing is mandatory at airports with low temperatures.
Main image - fresh water in or used water (amongst other unwanted matter) out?
You decide...
(all images Tyler McDowell)

Gate Guidance. Above - yellow lines show pilots the correct way around airports and below, at the gate; gate and stand number, the flight using it (Ryanair 1272) and the indicator below tells the pilot if he has the nosewheel on the taxi line *(Tyler McDowell)*

Ground Ops

Left - loading power; a mobile unit plugged into the aircraft nose.
Loading provisions; bags, food, water and all the other goodies found on a long haul flight.
Main image - cargo is one of an airline's big earners, with the holds most airliners having plenty of room for it as well as passenger's bags.
(all images Tyler McDowell)

4
Wind and Fire

There is just one life for each of us: our own

Euripides

KJ

There are airports and there are airports. For most travellers, particularly in the high-tech world of 2017, when flying between the big redeveloped terminals of today all airports look the same. Big spaces through which the multitudes pass, each deep in their own thoughts, thinking of the quickest way home, the business meeting at the other end, the holiday, where to get a cheap cup of coffee or tea - is there such a thing at airports these days? Perhaps surprisingly, yes. Although not everywhere; once cocooned in an airport terminal, most people are a captive group, left with no choice but to pay the price or go without. Human nature being what it is, any captured mass is ripe for plucking and airport prices, like some elsewhere, can be staggeringly high. Given the numbers flying today, it's to a degree inevitable that whilst many avoid confrontation and complaint, there are increasing numbers that will not keep quiet and will make their feelings known, either at the time or later. Many US airports and an increasing number in other countries are now insisting that vendors in their terminals charge the same price for their wares that they would charge in any street in any town.

Whatever the price of a cup of coffee, generally speaking, the developed nations of the world have the safest airports, and the same can be said for air space and airlines. The accident record for all three is outstanding. That record of transporting people from one place to another in almost complete safety is a testimony to the people whose job it is to make air travel as safe as it is. Despite the good record, there are airports everywhere that either have or had a reputation that, although standing up to scrutiny, had some individual aspects that made flying into them, and for that matter out of them as well, potentially more hazardous than others.

Hong Kong's old airport at Kai Tak, long since replaced by it's current mega-airport at Chep Lap Kok, was the famous one. With just one runway, aircraft either approached over the sea, which was fairly bland, or took off over it, which could be equally unremarkably dull. The other end was unique.

Arriving aircraft could not begin their approach some distance out and descend gracefully and in a straight line like at most airports. There were - are - others with strange approaches, some even more dramatic, but none that required all aircraft, from the smallest to the biggest, to approach with the runway on the right and then demand the pilots fling their aircraft into a tight right turn to line up and land right after coming out of the turn. It was said that one could almost reach out and take washing off the line strung out on the balconies of the apartment buildings just feet under the turning aircraft. The turn was needed because of Lion Rock, a substantial chunk of mountain at that end of the runway. A large red and white checkerboard sat on the side of the rock, almost screaming out loud to aircrew, 'Turn now'!

It was always a manoeuvre that left the unknowing and unready with sweaty palms. Kai Tak was the only really busy airport handling every type of aircraft from short range Boeing 737s and Airbus A320s up to the bloated shape of the 747 and even Concorde (not on scheduled services but the delta-winged rocket did visit Kai Tak), although it never handled the brobdingnagian Airbus A380 - watching one of those do the turn would have been the aviation geek's ecstasy moment.

Bad weather and high winds kept the game alive, making Kai Tak even more interesting, more challenging, and there were numerous instances of aircraft, even as big as a 747, arriving over the runway almost sideways. One either got straight real quick, or powered up, climbed away and tried again. The airport did have a remarkably good safety record however and there were no crashes on to the tall apartment blocks clustered around the base of Lion Rock. Kai Tak closed in 1998.

For scenic arrivals, departures and mountains all around, Innsbruck can be interesting. Even more so although on a much smaller scale, is St. Barts in the Caribbean — the hill at the runway's end means literally diving over it to land on the short runway. Winair and St Barts Commuter operate passenger flights with the De Havilland Twin Otter and the first-timer will probably find it an unsettling experience.

A similar method was used at Toncontin, the airport that serves the Honduran city of Tegucigalpa. With its proximity to mountainous terrain, its short runway, and its historically difficult approach to runway 02, requiring all aircraft up to a Boeing 757 (the largest allowed to fly in to the airport) to dive over a hill at the 02 end, Toncontin has always been considered a tricky airport to use. It does have a good safety record however and in May 2009, much of the hill was removed, the runway getting a short extension, making life much easier for flight crew and undoubtedly less worrisome for passengers

Possibly the ultimate airport for mountainous surroundings is Paro in the Himalayan Kingdom of Bhutan. The only place in which to put an airport lay at the bottom of a valley and arriving aircraft have to make numerous twists and turns while descending with the towering mountains seemingly a few feet from the wing tips, a procedure that has been described as terrifying for the unwary and those who have never been there. The airport does have an excellent safety record, as does the national airline of Bhutan, Druk Air, a testimony to the skill of the carrier's pilots who fly the Airbus A319 into Paro.

Berlin Tempelhof also presented a challenge although for entirely different reasons. Made famous by its role in the Berlin Airlift, the airport was always something of a curiosity. Known as the *Zentral Flughafen* in German, (Central Airport in English), the airport was one of the busiest pre-World War II and the Nazi regime wanted it to be a showcase for German aviation. Circular in shape, and almost in the middle of Berlin, (hence it's local moniker) its location meant that it was always surrounded by houses and apartment blocks. Even so, a huge (for its time) new terminal was built on its north-western side — a terminal that when built, had the largest unsupported roof in the world. Like most pre-war airfields, it had grass landing areas but after the war it became the headquarters of the US Air Force who built two parallel runways. As well as it's US Forces use, Tempelhof became the primary airport serving West Berlin, and with the eastern half of the city under Soviet control, the border was very close to the end of the airport's runways, which, since the size and rotund shape of the field remained as it was before the war, were very short, particularly for jet airliners. Air France moved to the more difficult to get to Tegel, in the northern part of West Berlin when they introduced the Caravelle, which needed the longer runways available there. Conveniently, Tegel also lay in what was then the French Sector of West Berlin.

The airliners of BEA/BA and Pan Am remained at Tempelhof, in the US sector of the city, first with propeller aircraft like the British Vickers Viscount and US built Douglas DC6, then with the jet powered BAC One-Eleven, which BEA called the Super One-Eleven, and Pan Am's Boeing 727s, serving the Internal German Service network of routes to other West German cities (National carrier Lufthansa were banned from serving Berlin at the time). Arriving flights were obliged to make a tight turn over East Berlin and then descend rapidly on to the longer of the two runways, 27 Left, still very short for a jet airliner, all of which had weight restrictions to enable them to take off on the strip of tarmac.

If the tricky descent wasn't enough, arriving airliners also had to contend with being buzzed occasionally by Russian fighters while on final approach, the trickiest part of any flight. All Berlin's air services moved to a rebuilt Tegel in 1975 although Tempelhof remained open until it closed for good in 2008 but it had a perfect safety record, although the cemetery at the end of 27 Left could, for passengers at least, be a little disquieting.

Tempelhof today is a park, the haunt of joggers and kite flyers, now the only flying to take place there.

Denver's Stapleton Airport, replaced on 28 February, 1995 (16 months behind schedule and at a cost of $4.8 billion, nearly $2 billion over budget), by the Colorado city's state-of-the-art, and much, much larger, field some distance out in the countryside, had a slightly unfortunate reputation for suffering from wind shear. Not called the 'Mile-high City' for nothing, Denver is indeed one mile above sea level, hence the nickname and the sometimes turbulent conditions around it. One of the attractions in the Rocky Mountains immediately west of the city itself is the grave of Buffalo Bill, or William Cody, to give him his correct name. A walk up the hill to the site does indeed leave the unknowing and unwary breathless due to the thin air. Cody started life as a mail rider for the Pony Express, later serving in the American civil war, then becoming a scout for the US Army during the Indian Wars. He then started 'Buffalo Bill's Wild West Show', tasking his performances on tour across the US and in 1887, to Great Britain and Europe. Following his death in Denver on 10 January 1917, he was buried on Lookout Mountain, overlooking the city where he spent his final days.

Stapleton Airport was the dream of City Mayor Ben F. Stapleton, who bought the land for $143,000 in the 1920s and to begin with, it was unkindly referred to as 'Stapleton's Folly'. The airport opened in October 1929 and located on the eastern edge of Denver, traffic figures grew continuously until it had become the fourth-busiest in the USA in terms of landings and take-offs, hardly a surprise since it had become a major hub for both United and Continental Airlines. With the arrival of jet airliners and bigger aircraft generally, Stapleton had become far too small but the derisory remarks concerning Ben Stapleton's folly had long been forgotten. Its accident rate was never as bad as it was occasionally made out to be and its heavy use belied the scare stories. It did have long runways due to the thin air but even so, it could get very windy one mile above sea level and in the lee of the Rocky Mountains.

Wind shear has been one of the deadliest weather-related conditions known to aviation. In June 1975, Eastern Airlines Flight 66, operated by a Boeing 727, made its final approach to JFK, New York. The weather that day was poor, with low cloud and gusting winds. As the flight neared the runway, a brief outburst of wind shear literally pulled the aircraft into the ground, the 727 crashing on to the approach lights and into Thurston Basin, a creek at the end of the runway. Sixteen people survived out of the 128 souls on board. The accident was the worst in the airport's history.

Eastern 66 was the defining moment in beginning to understand the full effects of wind shear but ten years after the accident, a Delta Airlines Lockheed TriStar met the same fate on final approach to Dallas/Ft. Worth in Texas. 133 people died. Wind shear can occur in good weather or bad and the decade between Eastern 66 and the Delta flight at Dallas directly resulted in the improvements to weather radar and wind shear detection, making it far less likely that wind shear today results in an

Wind and Fire

accident.

The island of St. Helena is famous for two things; one being its remoteness from everywhere else in the South Atlantic Ocean, some 1,200 miles west of the African mainland and 1,800 miles east from Brazil, and the second, because of the first, being the island to where Napoleon Bonaparte was banished after his defeat at the Battle of Waterloo. Bonaparte had earlier escaped a similar exile from the Mediterranean island of Elba – his second exile was far enough away from everywhere to make another escape virtually impossible and he died on St. Helena in May 1891.

Even today, getting to the island means a lengthy sea journey and despite the construction of a brand new airport, the sea trip remains. The airport is complete, and theoretically at least open for business, but because its location on the island means it suffers very badly from wind shear, no commercial airline is willing to use it. Test flights with a Boeing 737 have shown that to use the airport for regular passenger flights means a trying task for pilots to maintain control on final approach and the likelihood of a wind shear-induced crash is high, to the point of the airport being unsafe to use. Until a solution is found (if it can be), it will still take a long voyage by ship to reach St. Helena.

There is a well-established school of thought that suggests to pilots that, when arriving over a runway to land, one needs to get the wheels on the deck and slow safely to taxi speed as rapidly as possible, a methodology that does work but occasionally leads to hard landings and some discomfort for passengers. The ultimate landing for pilots is the 'greaser', the gentle touchdown with nary the merest bounce or bump. To do it however, requires consummate skill, clear, fine weather, no crosswind and a very long runway. It is not unknown for pilots to attempt a greaser and end up touching down late, resulting in heavy braking lest the aircraft runs out of tarmac. Most passengers never know the difference between heavy braking and the lighter touch but other pilots on board will and so will regular fliers.

As mentioned in the last chapter, aircraft brakes generate a lot of heat when used heavily and I can bear witness to the effect of heavy braking; on occasion, an aircraft will 'float' after the initial contact between runway and main wheels. Some aircraft can be more prone to it than others but when it happens there is a gentle bounce on first contact before the aircraft remains in the air, although only a few feet above the runway. With not enough power to actually fly yet still not on the ground, the runway rapidly gets shorter - and shorter.

It has happened. Not frequently however, pilots generally are too well trained and disciplined but a Lockheed L1011 TriStar at Leeds some years ago 'floated' after main gear contact and finally had all its wheels on the runway too far along to stop before over-running and sliding down a slope beyond the runway's end. Other than a collapsed nose wheel, there was little damage and everybody walked away. At Gatwick in 1994 I photographed a Nigeria Airways Cargo Boeing 707 as it made its final approach past the terminal and observation deck before gently touching down right where it was supposed to. The 707 then floated for nearly half the length of the runway before eventually settling on the tarmac but the presumably full application of brakes saw a huge plume of grey smoke emerge from the wheels. Just how powerful aircraft brakes really are was demonstrated by the aircraft leaving the runway on to the taxiway turn off well before the runway's end but whilst it was still on the runway, Gatwick's Fire Services vehicles were already out of their station and chasing after the aircraft.

As I and other spectators watched from the distant roof top viewing deck, the aircraft was surrounded by the fire service equipment as the wheels were watched

Gatwick 1994

A Nigeria Airways Cargo Boeing 707 makes a seemingly normal touchdown but 'floats' for too long before finally settling on the runway...

the resultant heavy braking sees a plume of grey smoke from the overheating wheels and the fire service vehicles emerge from their station...

the aircraft exits the runway on to the taxiway turn-off and is surrounded by the emergency services as they watch for fire...

after a few moments, the aircraft is escorted to its parking stand with no problems; just a floater along the runway, a moment of brief drama and a slight delay for other flights.

(all images Kevan James)

carefully for fire. There was none. A moment of brief drama. A delay for other aircraft but no crash. Just the result of a floater along the runway. *Get it on the deck…all wheels on the runway, keep it straight and slow to safe taxi speed…*

Nigeria Airways went out of business not long after and the 707 was finally retired from use around the same time.

∎

5
Stacked Decks

But perhaps, when you sleep, you will dream of me

Shira Anthony

KJ
How many people once stood on an airport observation deck, usually found on the roof of the airport terminal? The question's key word is 'once'. The answer may be a little surprising but at least in days gone by, more than one might think. The obvious are those with the interest to do so, camera or notebook (sometimes both), in hand, snapping away at what arrives and noting the aircraft registrations. But the most common visitors to airport observation decks were always the 'meeters, greeters and weepers' – relatives and friends of those travelling somewhere. In times past, air travel was for the wealthy but every airport had somewhere for the traveller's escorts to watch the departure or arrival. Not too far behind, in numbers at least, were those who visited the local airport not because they were necessarily enthusiastic about aircraft but simply because it was a day out and a visit to somewhere different. In the case of the now long gone International Arrivals Building (IAB) at New York, it was to have dinner in the classy restaurant that once occupied a prominent position inside the building – no fast food here. This was a place were finely dressed waiters offered a premium service to equally finely dressed patrons. There were similar establishments in many airport terminals around the world. The airport terminal was a showcase for the cities they served. Some made loud statements about the vision of planners and architects, others more simple but functional even so and all reflected the era in which they were built. The airport was an attraction in its own right. 1940s and '50s Art Deco abounded – Washington National Airport (today known as Ronald Reagan National) serving the capital city of the USA, and Liverpool, home of The Beatles being two good examples. Both terminals shared the same elements of style although both very different. The two buildings continue to exist; Washington is still in use although much modified and extended. Liverpool's is now a hotel, the entire airport having shifted south when its present runway, hugging the banks of the River Mersey, was opened, later followed by the terminal in use today. Its original terminal is now somewhat divorced from the airport but preserved as a historic landmark. The old runways are long gone but the ramp in front of the hotel is still there and occupied by a small number of equally preserved aircraft – unlike some, the City of Liverpool does not forget its heritage easily.

There is a perception that airliner enthusiasts are a minority but air travel provokes simply because it exists. The same can be said about airports. Controversial today undoubtedly but essential transport infrastructure even so and always the haunt of the aviation minded. Every airport had its observation deck - Germany's terminals had their *Besucher Terrasse*, or Visitor's Terrace, Heathrow had the Roof Gardens and in Cyprus, Nicosia's 1968-built terminal had an open air viewing deck running along its length – I remember standing on it and watching a Middle East Airlines Caravelle arrive and an RAF VC10 depart *(oh, for a good camera and the know-how to use it back then…)*. The Pan American Terminal's Boeing 747 extension at JFK may have had its roof intended (and used) as a car park but however unintentional, also provided an excellent place to watch the comings and goings on the airport's longest runway right in front of it. The most vibrant time for airliner observing was the late 1960s and early 1970s – classic jetliners like the Boeing 707, 727 and 737 and the Douglas

DC8 and DC9 were in widespread use, Soviet-built Tupolevs and Ilyushins arrived and departed mysteriously, the French built Caravelle, and even the world's first jet airliner, the Comet could still be seen, their jet engines undoubtedly deafening but there were also plenty of propliners around; the Vickers Viscount and Vanguard, even some earlier types like the Bristol Britannia and the Douglas DC6 and 7, not to mention the ubiquitous DC3 and if you were lucky, the occasional Lockheed Electra. Dominating them all was the then-new Boeing 747, the Jumbo Jet. As the 1970s wore inexorably on, the 747 was joined by the Lockheed L1011 TriStar and Douglas DC10, smaller than the Boeing but still massively larger than the rest. All could be seen from the deck on top of the airport terminal, almost any terminal, almost anywhere.

All of that said, it might also be worth asking why so many people (and there are serious numbers around the world, on every continent) are so enthusiastic and wanting to take so many photographs of airliners? For that matter, the same applies to military aircraft; the answer is the same – a passion for the subject. Everybody has their passions, their interests. Talk to an avid collector of stamps and they will willingly talk for hours about their subject, and demonstrate the extensive collection they may well have spent years accumulating. In the days of film it was a little harder for the photography enthusiast to follow their passion since it cost a huge amount to buy a camera – not to mention additional equipment to help improve their techniques and thus their pictures – but also to develop, process and print the results; it's the main reason why it took me so long to become a serious photographer.

The digital revolution was just that; a revolution. Suddenly, once one had a camera and a computer (a big enough expenditure of themselves) the world was one's oyster. No longer was one limited to thirty-six images on a roll of film and the cost of making pictures out of them; no longer did one have to worry about wasted images if the result was not what was hoped for. And with the camera phone, everybody today can simply snap away to their heart's content – and they do, as the images that appear on social media are ample evidence of.

But at the same time, places at which one can take photographs have become ever more restricted. Despite that there are still numerous official spotting areas at a number of airports around the world, at most German airports, at Amsterdam and Zurich and elsewhere. Having found one's official area, many are also good for photography, although it depends on what one actually wants to photograph.

One school of thought suggests that the perfect aircraft picture is a side profile with nothing in the background and nothing around the subject. If one wants the perfect airliner portrait, that's okay; some of the finest photographs in the world fall in this category but there is also a case to be made for ramp action, with an airliner in the midst of its turn-round, doors open and lots of bustle, making the image an active one. The same applies to the dramatic take-off shot, in fine or foul weather, or the smoky result of the impact of tyres on tarmac as the aircraft touches down. For the more expansive look, an airport panorama can also make for a spectacular image with a wide-angle lens capturing the overall view. For many however, the lack of on-airport facilities means spending time at the end of a runway and catching the aircraft on final approach. There are thousands of excellent images taken by thousands of talented photographers of this kind of airliner picture but a ground-to-air shot of something with only the sky (cloudy or brilliant blue) in the background could be taken anywhere. This doesn't necessarily detract from the quality of the image and the photographer knows where they were when they shot the picture. Even so, an 'airport' photo needs something to identify the location somewhere in the image.

There is a well established tradition of aircraft spotting in the UK, the USA, across much of Western Europe and elsewhere, like Japan, but it is not universally so. There are some countries where it is less recognized, perhaps due to cultural differences but often because of military concerns. Many airports share their runways with local air force units, like the German Air Force Transport squadron at Cologne. Shared use of that kind doesn't usually present much of an issue but if the air force unit consists of anything else, problems can arise. There are numerous instances of enthusiasts from the UK travelling somewhere to spend time at an airport and ending up staring at the inside of a police station cell and facing some hard (and occasionally brutal) questions as to why they are pointing a camera at the airfield, Greece being one example. Yet the contradictions can be quite marked. Athens' old airport, Hellenikon, just eight miles from the city centre, was something of a magnet for spotters, with one hotel right by the runway threshold offering spotter's breaks and a rooftop bar from where numerous images were taken without any problems. The island of Skiathos is a well established tourist destination and its airport is sometimes referred to as the 'St Maarten of Greece' the runway being almost identical to the Caribbean island, separated only from the sea by a public road. Consequently it is a popular place for plane spotting and there are no reported conflicts with the local authorities.

Tourism has always played a vital role in Greece's economy and it is undeniably a beautiful country. Yet a visit to some of the less well known airports around has been known to cause problems – especially if the military are also based at the airport. The problem becomes more noticeable in some Middle Eastern and African countries, where air transport enthusiasm is less well understood.

There is a simple answer; check before travelling. You might not get what you want but on the other hand a visit or call to the Embassy of the country you want to visit can bring some very encouraging results and advance arrangements might bring its own rewards. That applies even more today that it did yesterday; security concerns are now one of air transport's overriding issues and even where spotting and airliner photography has been allowed before, it may not be now – with plenty of precedent for terrorist atrocities, things are not what they once were. The airport observation deck does still exist and there are a few, but not everywhere. Where an airport does have official viewing areas, stick to it and don't wander around unescorted. If asked to move, move.

Put more bluntly, use a little common sense and don't put either yourself or others at risk by not thinking or for that matter, not co-operating with authority when asked to do so.

Observation
Paradise

Top right - most German airports, Cologne being one, have their Observation Decks but the go-to airport in Europe is Amsterdam, centre left and right, where the Panorama Terrace gives good views. *(Tyler McDowell)*
Lower right - a sunny summer afternoon at Myrtle Avenue, just off the threshold of Heathrow's runway 27 left can also be a relaxing time. *(Kevan James)*
Main Image - another must-visit airport is Zurich, which has its deck and an apron bus tour. *(Flughafen Zurich AG)*

6
The Cabbie

Is life not a hundred times too short for us to stifle ourselves?

Friedrich Nietzsche

KJ
There is a wonderfully revealing scene early in the movie, *'Coogan's Bluff'*, in which Clint Eastwood plays the role of an Arizona Sheriff, the Coogan of the title, who is sent to New York to pick up a runaway fugitive. Coogan arrives in New York and, with Cowboy Hat and boots, is obviously not a native. After arriving from JFK on the New York Airways helicopter service to the heliport on top of the Pan Am building, he gets a taxi to the Manhattan police station where he has arranged to see Detective McIlroy (Lee J. Cobb) and as he gets out of the taxi, the driver tells him the fare. Coogan then asks how many Macy's Stores there are in New York. Puzzled the driver replies, 'One. Why?'

Laconically, Coogan replies, 'We passed it twice...' The driver smiles, realising he has been caught out but still charges the same fare - $2.95, 'including the charge for baggage'. Since Coogan has only a briefcase as it is due to be a one-day stay, he hands over $3, 'including the tip'.

For the most part, taxi drivers are honest and a mine of information about the place they earn their living, will get you where you want to go quickly, safely and the fare will be what the meter says. But there are always a few...my dad knew Paris well and on one occasion had reason for a taxi ride and gently pointed out to the driver that they were going the long way, and thus the more expensive way, to his destination.

Like Coogan's cabbie, the French one smiled but charged a lower fare, reality dawning that my dad was no mere tourist. It happened to me once too, in Bournemouth of all places. The UK south coast town is a holiday resort and full of visitors in the summer, me being one. I was there for a sports event held on the outskirts of the town and a half-hour ride from my hotel. Fortunately I have a good sense of direction and I'm very good with maps so I knew where to go and the cab ride out was quick and cheap. One the way back it was a different matter. This time, the driver took the scenic route but part way through the journey, as we chatted, I dropped a hint or two and the driver lopped the fare in half when we got back to my hotel - like father, like son and the driver knew he had been rumbled. Heathrow at one time had a slightly unfortunate reputation with Japanese tourists waving fistfuls of pound notes around and, not speaking a word of English, were charged those fistfuls for their trips into London. Stand out from the crowd and you may be a victim. It is, up to a point, human nature to try it on with the unwary. Even so, most people are still honest. Including taxi drivers.

The Port Authority bus station in Manhattan has been described in a variety of ways, one of the more polite being hell on earth, and having been deposited there by the bus from JFK, having arrived from London earlier, although I knew where my hotel was, it was a longish walk carrying bags (like I said, stand out from the crowd...). A spell on duty there for a Port Authority Police Officer is reputedly not the first choice of most but since there was one, I asked. His reply was get a cab but from the official rank outside on the street and not from one of the characters hanging around inside asking if anybody wants a cab. Advice duly taken even though I'm not that stupid but its always worth checking. Fifteen minutes later I am safe and sound and where I'm supposed to be.

The Cabbie

For my trip back to JFK as I left the hotel (looking the part of the visiting traveller and a very young one at that; shoulder bag and carrying a suitcase in one hand – a chicken ripe for plucking), a man leaning casually by the hotel entrance asked me if I wanted a cab. I asked where his vehicle was and he indicated a bright yellow New York medallion cab parked by the hotel entrance. Since he had a medallion I asked how much the fare would be to JFK. Depending on traffic, the reply was a fair fare so I also asked him which route he would take. There are two; the most heavily used, under the east river and the vagaries of the notorious Van Wyck, or, perverse as it might seem, north, and in the opposite direction to JFK towards La Guardia Airport, then doubling back on oneself to get to JFK. The Van Wyck being what it is and New York traffic being what it is, the second route is often the quickest and thus, for the passenger, the cheapest, even though the Triborough Bridge, over which one must cross, is a toll bridge, the toll payable by the passenger. The bridge, a 1934 colossus (there are numerous bridges around the USA that can be called the same – think San Francisco and the Golden Gate) has its tolls rooted in the long distant memories of times past and of the Port Authority of New York and New Jersey's (PANYNJ) formation. Many US highways carry the name 'turnpike' and do so as a toll had to be paid - a turnpike was a Seventeenth Century English device that contained wooden pikes blocking the highway and would not be turned and thus opened until Ye Toll was paid. The PANYNJ was formed to raise funds to build and operate the highways, tunnels, bridges, docks and harbours, and eventually the airports, serving the New York and New Jersey area. The tolls were supposed to pay for those highways, tunnels, bridges and the rest, and would cease to be levied once the construction costs had been paid. So why are they still in place, since the costs were done and dusted decades before? It is a never-ending gravy train - the tolls are paid because they are there and simply because they exist people will sit in their cars on traffic-clogged highways paying for the privilege of doing so, including those in a taxi.

Traffic does at least flow across the Triborough so it's still cheaper than being stuck in traffic not flowing with the meter ticking. This guy seemed to know his business and described the second way so let's rock 'n' roll, and try to beat the Van Wyck. Plenty have tried, none have succeeded.

Those who have never been to New York, or for that matter anywhere in the USA, may well be aware of the less palatable aspects of its reputation. Hollywood doesn't help sometimes but New York is like any big city the world over. It has good parts and bad parts and mostly good people. One of New York's most famous assets is Central Park, the huge oblong of greenery that sits right in the middle of Manhattan. Either side is lined with museums and expensive apartment buildings; its southern end meets the centre of the city and its skyscrapers. It is the part seen in the brochures, events going on, the zoo and people sunbathing in the summer, skating on the lake in winter. The north end however is, or was in 1986, overgrown and conventional wisdom suggested not going there, especially after dark. Beyond the park's northern end is Harlem - back to Hollywood again; when Roger Moore made his debut as James Bond in *'Live and Let Die'* he gets a taxi to chase a villain and the route takes them north. As they drive through the Park, the driver says, 'Hey man, you sure you know where you goin'? You're headin' into Harlem!'

Stony-faced, Bond replies, 'Just keep on the tail of that juke-box and there's an extra twenty in it for you....'

After an encounter with the villain and being rescued by a local CIA agent, the agent says, 'You sure know how to draw attention to yourself, Bond – a white face in Harlem.'

Bruce Willis had to do something even more flamboyant in the 1995 movie *'Die Hard with a Vengeance '*, a sequence also set in Harlem. But this is where a good cabbie is like gold and this one was happy to chat and point out places and things. You want real black culture? Go to Harlem. You want great music, played live? Go to Harlem (the same applies in New Orleans – real jazz abounds and my dad and I did; we listened entranced in a club in the heart of the southern city and we were the only white people there. Nobody minded or treated us differently simply because we were white).

Harlem is a part of New York that is heavily populated by people whose skin colour just happens to be black but like most people everywhere, as friendly and welcoming as any and proud of their city. So was my cabbie. He told me he would probably make better money looking for business outside hotels in Manhattan, although not all were for trips out to JFK. When he gets one, like me today, if he was lucky he would pick up a fare back. If not, he would return to Manhattan empty and look for more work. He lived not far from La Guardia so knew the roads as well as anybody. Like the traditional London black cab Driver Licence and the vehicle itself, a New York Cabbie's yellow Medallion cab and the licence to go with it can be hard to get and easy to lose. Get people where they need to go in reasonable time and in one piece, you can earn your living. Don't and you won't.

The fare came to exactly what he said it would, and I gave him an extra ten dollars. The educational ride was worth it.

∎

7
UK Wings I

If you're not having fun, you're doing something wrong

Groucho Marx

KJ
The late 1980s and early 1990s were a fascinating and educational time for me as I spent them jetting back and forth across the Atlantic, with London Gatwick becoming very familiar along with the city of Dallas and its giant airport, first with British Caledonian, followed by British Airways once the two had merged (in truth it was more of a takeover) and then Northwest, this time via Minneapolis St. Paul, or MSP.

MSP was interesting. The first time I arrived there two things struck me; the first was that it retained a very traditional US look to it and secondly, it had a claim to fame since it had the lead role in the 1969 movie, *'Airport'*, also starring Burt Lancaster, Dean Martin, Jean Seberg, George Kennedy and Van Heflin. The movie was…is…one of the three most influential of my life, the other two being *'Battle of Britain'* (made around the same time and with an all-star cast) and much later, *'The Final Countdown'*, with Kirk Douglas and Martin Sheen. Those last two had nothing to do with commercial aviation, one being 1940s military and the other 1980s military - as much as I may have an ongoing love affair with, and married to, airports and airliners, my mistresses are however, the Spitfire, Hurricane, ME109 and Heinkel 111, plus the Grumman Tomcat, along with sundry other US Navy aircraft. On a more patriotic note, I should also throw in the Royal Air Force and the Fleet Air Arm, the Meteor, the Hunter and Harrier, Jaguar and Tornado, along with numerous other British aircraft (even allowing for those built with European partners).

But MSP is where it all began, with that movie. Airline names and colour schemes had changed but the airport still looked like an airport. Home to Northwest (NWA), the famous red tails were everywhere and with NWA having merged, or taken over if one prefers, Republic Airlines, also MSP based, it made NWA the dominant carrier at Minneapolis. Connecting there to both Dallas and Los Angeles was easy and swift despite having to use both MSP's terminals; the two are separated by an active runway, upon which the 747 from London had landed. International arrivals are at the Hubert Humphrey Terminal and a short bus ride takes one over to the main building, used in the movie and named the Lindbergh Terminal, after one of Minnesota's most famous sons since the man himself was born not far from here. Hubert Humphrey was a local man who rose to become US Vice-President.

The routine was broken in December 1988 by using Pan Am from Heathrow to New York and going on to San Antonio, with a plane change at Dallas Ft. Worth, to American Airlines for the last leg. Two weeks after departing New York and returning to London, Lockerbie happened. It was the beginning of the end for Pan Am. The already financially bereft industry veteran struggled on for another two years but the question was when the end would come, not if. Pan Am was a huge name in the airline world and many people thought the worst would not happen. Even when the airline entered Chapter 11 Bankruptcy Protection in the USA (designed to allow a company time to re-organise itself without being hounded by its creditors), the belief was that, as such an American institution, a way would be found to emerge from its difficulties. *'It won't happen…not to Pan Am'*.

Then it did happen and almost overnight, on 5 December, 1991. Pan Am's final was a Boeing 727 from Barbados to Miami, named *Clipper Goodwill*. A little ironic perhaps, since the historic carrier seemed to receive little of that during those final two years.

No airline had quite the impact or influence that Pan American World Airways had, except possibly BOAC. Other airlines have gone bust just as any business can and does. But the downfall of Pan Am was different. Granted its founder, Juan Trippe, was not everybody's cup of tea and he was quite content to use his own influence with friends in high places to further the interests of his airline but has any other left the airways as Pan American did? Has there been another airline like Pan Am and has a similar void been left by the departure? Other companies have their memorials and even the TWA terminal still stands at JFK - but not the Pan Am Worldport.

Twenty-five years on, nothing is left of the airline and as mentioned above, there was little of the empathy towards Pan Am that other failing carriers received when they went broke. After Juan Trippe retired, there is little doubt that the airline was poorly led for some time; questionable decisions were made in a number of areas, all of which contributed to the airline's eventual failure. Management was perhaps guilty of taking the name for granted, believing that merely because the company existed and had history, all things would be given to them. Real life however, can less predictable and status, once earned, can be lost and lost very quickly.

And yet...and yet...Pan Am might have survived. Thomas Plaskett had become its chairman in 1988 and had instituted changes that were working. The airline was expanding and took over the terminal next to the Worldport at JFK for its domestic services, to where I arrived from Dallas that December in 1988. Originally built for Braniff, the design was very different from the Worldport, more boxy, more traditional and perhaps less imaginative, but comfortable even so. A connecting walkway was nearing completion linking the two terminals and there was optimism around the airline.

Just two weeks later there came Lockerbie.

The other change to what had become a regular route to Dallas came before the tragedy of Lockerbie and the final end for Pan Am, earlier that year, in February 1988, when Air New Zealand, after opening a new route from Auckland to Honolulu, Dallas and London, were in the midst of promoting themselves. With their expansion in mind, I was able to fly them on the Gatwick-Dallas-Gatwick sector, including a cockpit visit and travelling business class...unaccustomed luxury for one normally a cattle class traveller. The only missing part was not being able to fly further and go all the way to Auckland with them.

I also managed to fit in two UK short-haul trips from Heathrow to East Midlands on British Midland Airways, Jersey on BA, using one of the airline's long-serving BAC111s, Los Angeles twice, and Amsterdam, my first visit there since my teen years. Jersey once more (my Mother lived there for a while) and the last trip of the era saw me use Boston for the one and only time, on my back to London from my second visit to Los Angeles. Using Northwest again, the flight was supposed to route via MSP but for some reason (I never did find out why – I should have asked) the leg to MSP was cancelled and passengers re-booked by NWA to return to London via Boston instead. It did add another airport to the list however.

It was a fun time and all of it work-related. I wasn't being paid much, not enough to photograph as much as I would have wanted to but at least it was doing something that got me on planes flying.

UK Wings I

As good as it had been, there comes a time when one has to stop merely having fun, grow up, get mature and be a responsible citizen. I've never quite got the hang of any of them except possibly the last…even so, the past few years had been hugely rewarding but I had to settle down and do a proper job.

One can get a little blasé about jetting back and forth across the Atlantic as I had been doing but my trip to Dallas in 1992 was to be my last. Real life was about to get in the way and it meant moving to the Midlands and away from Heathrow and Gatwick to do a proper job – one has to go where the work is. I would at least be spending my time designing and producing event programmes and magazines, writing and editing them and to a degree at least, working with news media people, although none of it was aviation related. Even though London and its airports would be further away, it was a step along the road to where I wanted to go.

LHR-JFK
December 1988

One of the most significant Decembers in commercial aviation history...

Above left - Pan Am's Boeing 747 *'Clipper Empress of the Skies'* rests at New York's John F. Kennedy after arriving from London.
Above right - circular rainbows and shadows on the clouds.
Centre right - descent over Long Island.
Lower right - final approach to JFK and shadows on the ground.
Main image - touchdown and rollout past the former Eastern Airlines terminal, now long since demolished, its user also part of aviation's past.
As is Pan American World Airways.
(all images Kevan James)

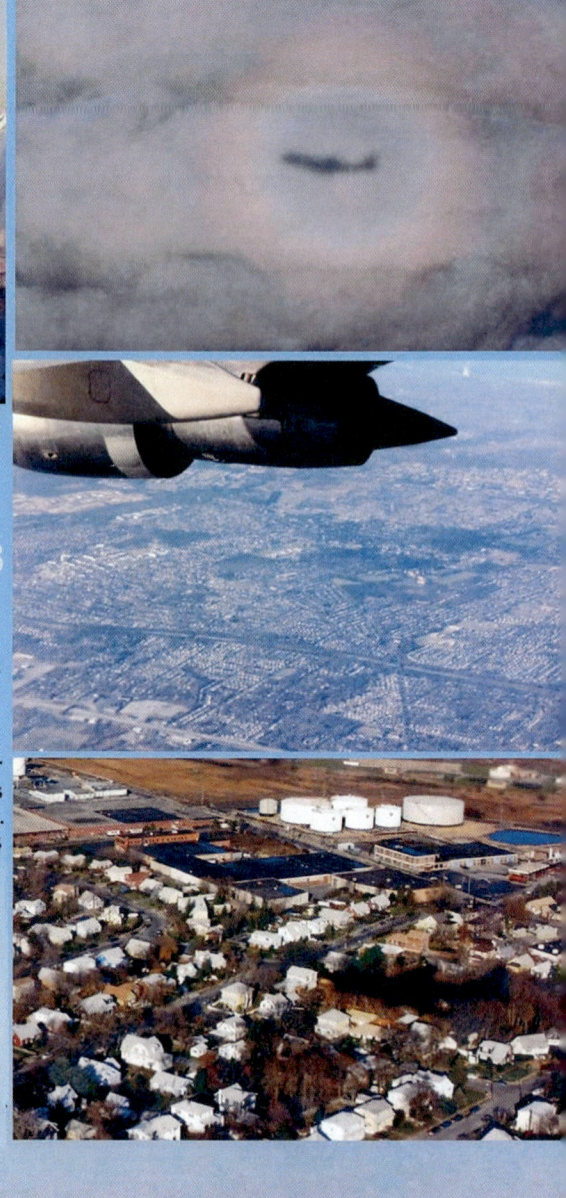

DALLAS/FT.WORTH

1988 again...
Left - the eye of the beholder; on board a British Caledonian Douglas DC10-30 arriving from Gatwick as a Lufthansa Boeing 747-230 does the same from Frankfurt.
Below left - part of the north cargo area.
Below right - one of the four terminals then in use. Today, there are five.
Main image - from the outside in and the inside out; faces at the window.
(all images Kevan James)

London Gatwick to Dallas/ Ft Worth (and back)

British Caledonian, then British Airways and Northwest were the airlines of choice for numerous journeys between the USA and the UK in the late 1980s and 1990s. London Gatwick, Dallas Fort Worth and Minneapolis St. Paul became familiar airports *(all images Kevan James)*

Minneapolis St. Paul
Minnesota

MSP

MSP was home to Northwest and the airline the primary user. The airport's biggest claim to fame was in 1969 when it was the setting for the movie 'Airport'. Northwest Airlines may have gone, having merged with Delta but although modified, the main terminal is still recognisable today as the one that became a movie superstar - and a star that became a defining influence on countless aviation-mad young minds...including the photographer.
(all images Kevan James)

Minnesota
Minneapolis MSP

Top four images - 1990s activity.
(Kevan James)
Lower left - the original Hubert Humphrey International Terminal, now replaced by a larger, state-of-the-art facility. Main image - the main terminal, named 'The Lindbergh Terminal', and seen in 1962, looking little different to its role in the movie seven years later.
(both images courtesy of the Metropolitan Airports Commission)

MINNEAPOLIS-SAINT PAUL INTERNATIONAL AIRPORT

Los Angeles late 1980s

From the moment they rose majestically in the centre of the airport, the arches of LAX's theme building became an iconic symbol of Southern California's air transport hub. The airport remains today a very busy place and a routine stop on trans-pacific air routes
(all images Kevan James)

Los Angeles in the 90s

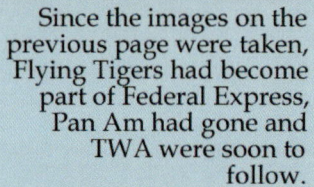

Since the images on the previous page were taken, Flying Tigers had become part of Federal Express, Pan Am had gone and TWA were soon to follow.
Los Angeles however, remains one of the the busiest airports in both the USA and the world.
(all images Kevan James)

Above left -
Arriving at Boston's Logan International, the city centre's proximity to the airport is quickly apparent.
Above right -
Pan Am still had a little time left before eventual closure.

Centre Right - Delta departing

Lower right -
"No Madam, this plane is not going to Denver..."
A common mistake by those who are unaware some airlines name their aircraft.

main image -
The eye-catching control tower, one of Logan's most noticable features.

(all images Kevan James)

BOS
Massachusetts

Channel Sunrise (Kevan James)

8
UK Wings II

A holiday for you would be to get on a plane and go somewhere, spend a day looking at the airport and taking photographs of it, then come back home

Lynda James

KJ

February 2002 - Given the time between now and my last sojourn into the wild blue yonder, it's not a surprise that Heathrow had seen some changes. One of them was the apparently never-ending stream of British Airways Airbus A319s and American Airlines Boeing 777s landing on runway 27 right as I watched from the domestic pier of Terminal 1. Another was British Midland Airways, who, despite the name, were now at the point where they were British Airways biggest UK European and domestic competitor at LHR (Virgin were still centred on Gatwick) and the aircraft colours were changing. Many of the airline's Boeing 737s now carried an interim livery, with the diamond shaped logo of the 1980s giving way to a temporary one. The airline had begun to style themselves as simply 'BMI', they now had a hangar at LHR, most of their operations ran from the London airport and they were soon to unveil a brighter blue, white and red scheme, with the Union Flag in a two-tone blue across the fin; perhaps something of a dig at British Airways, whose colourful but less than well-received world image fins were still in plentiful supply at LHR.

My destination however was not some far-flung corner of the globe but a more mundane and much shorter trip to Manchester (MAN) with BMI. The rocket-like performance of the 737-500, with the same engines as its longer brethren the 737-400, was quite something. Since the 737-500 had a much shorter fuselage, and thus less weight, the engines do give it some kick on take-off. The weather for February was remarkably kind although some turbulence midway through the short flight did result in the Captain announcing that he had requested a higher altitude to get out of it. Duly granted, the 737 rapidly gained height and a smoother passage, much to the relief of most of the passengers.

Manchester had become the UK's third busiest airport and its terminals have grown, been remodelled and two new ones built since my early days and the PR information the airport had been kind enough to send me for a school project. Its original terminal was still there, much refurbished and to its north, Terminal 2 stretches away from the car park's top floor which also serves as an official spotting point (one can also actually park cars there as well). MAN's newest terminal is just to the original building's left as you face the airfield and unfortunately can only be examined by those using it to fly somewhere. What sets Manchester apart from other UK airports however, as well as the top floor of the car park, is the equally official viewing park. Located immediately south of the terminals, not only is it close to the parallel taxiway that serves the airport's primary runway, but two viewing mounds provide over-the-fence views and the arrival of a 747 means the wing tip seems extraordinarily close. But it does give a good view.

Departure back to London saw an Airbus A320 in use, my first trip on one and the aircraft is painted in the Star Alliance scheme. Like all members, BMI had at least one aircraft carrying the logos of each airline in membership so it does make the ride a little different.

I can also say with complete honesty that despite its reputation to the contrary, it does not always rain in Manchester; as with my arrival, this day was clear and sunny. Departing to the south, one can even see (just) Liverpool and its airport in the distance. London and the south-east however is overcast and very windy. Approaching LHR over London, one is aware of the strong, gusting conditions buffeting the aircraft as the A320 emerges from the cloud and even though most passengers may not be aware of it, I can feel the pilot flying the aircraft right down to the runway and touchdown.

'Get it on the deck…all wheels on the runway, keep it straight and slow to safe taxi speed…'

Great flying, great landing…no attempt at a greaser. Just a smooth, safe touchdown.

FJ

I have always liked photography. I had liked planes for a long time, too, but somehow the two didn't 'meet' until spring 2014; instead I had always aimed my cameras at ships (growing up on the Isle of Wight meant I took more than a passing interest in the local maritime scene, full of cargo ships, tankers, ferries, liners and warships, etc.), animals and birds of the feathered, rather than the metal, variety. I was a semi-regular visitor to the old Queens Building at Heathrow in the 1990s, up until the sad day when the powers-that-be closed the viewing area post-9/11; however, I was content to just watch the activity, rather than photograph it. Unfortunately, since the Queens Building closed I had no reason to visit Heathrow further, apart from catching flights, until 2014.

So how did I eventually reconcile my liking for photography and my liking for planes? I have always loved travel and I have flown to the USA, South America, Asia and Australia on numerous occasions but it wasn't until a trip to Australia in 2014 that a hitherto latent aviation photography interest began to stir…I was on Cockatoo island in Sydney Harbour and there was a seemingly endless succession of Qantas 747s, among others, taking off from the nearby airport. I took a few bad photos and then forgot about it for the next couple of weeks. However, on the journey home, while in the terminal and taxiing out for departure, I started to really look at the planes and worked out the differences between, for example, a Boeing 777 and an Airbus A330. This was partly the result of a discussion on Facebook, when I took a photo of the Malaysia Airlines plane that was to take me to Kuala Lumpur en route to London and posted it on my timeline. Some of my friends were convinced it was a Boeing 777, some thought it was a Boeing 767 while others thought it was an Airbus A330 (it was an A330). Back then, I wasn't sure of the differences between them myself but with some observation it soon became apparent what was what - twin jets may look the same but they aren't and the Boeing 777 has become my favourite plane, along with the fabulous 747; the latter, sadly, is rapidly vanishing as four engines are less fuel-efficient than two.

This had awakened something because, when I got back to the UK, all I thought about was planes! I found myself staring skywards at everything up there, which made hanging out my washing on a sunny day a longer chore than it normally would have been as I was continually consulting Flight Radar 24 on my iPhone every time I heard a jet. Because of this, I found myself looking on a hotel website and I booked a night at Jury's Inn, Hatton Cross, at the end of May 2014 for a day of photography at Heathrow, specifically the now well-known spot at Myrtle Avenue, which has gained fame as the best place to watch aircraft since the demise of the Queens Building.

Myrtle Avenue is an otherwise unremarkable cul-de-sac off Hatton Road but on any day when the winds are coming from the west and the aircraft are landing on the southern runway (27L), particularly on a pleasant summer day, it - or more specifically, the grassy open space between Myrtle Avenue itself and the A30 - will be full of people enjoying the plane activity as a succession of airliners, large and small, pass close by on their way to landing on 27L.

Personally, this first visit was the beginning of what has become an all-consuming interest, some would say obsession, although I tend to think it more of the blossoming of a dormant seed. Why it never flowered before I don't know, but that's the way things go sometimes and aviation, specifically aviation photography, along with astronomy is my main interest these days. I think that, if my late father was still with us, it might have grown sooner, as he was a commercial pilot but, sadly, he passed away when I was two years old.

Since that day at Myrtle, I have been back many times to Heathrow to take photos, from different vantage points - unfortunately though, the fence has been double skinned and photographers and 'spotters' chased away by security, so no more line up or touch down shots are possible. This was thanks to a bunch of 'professional protesters' who broke in and staged a sit in on one of the runways in protest at airport expansion plans.

No matter what your views on air travel, there is a right way and a wrong way to do things, and these people did it the wrong way. In any case, they have made things awkward not only for airport authorities but for enthusiasts, too. That said, though, if you are content with 'sky shots' - and let's face it, planes are machines of the sky, it's their element - then you can do worse than a few hours spent near Heathrow.

That first visit to Myrtle Avenue was an eye opener as to just how popular this is as a hobby. I was struck by what a broad appeal it has, as then and on various trips since, I have noticed that spotting and photography appeals to all age ranges, both sexes and all walks of life. I think the general public believe it is a pastime, along with other niche interests such as birdwatching or astronomy, reserved for socially-awkward middle-aged men who still live with their mothers, but that's far from the case. A lot of my aviation friends are ordinary people with jobs and, in most cases, families, over a wide variety of ages from teens to retired, and while women don't outnumber the men they are far from absent from the scene; in fact on one trip to Heathrow back in 2015, when I met up with some friends, there were four of us and three were women. It's actually quite a wide demographic and this makes it vibrant and interesting – perhaps far more so than the very small ship enthusiast scene, which does have an elderly and mostly male following.

I have since travelled to other airports in Europe - Dublin, Manchester, London Luton, Birmingham, Amsterdam and Frankfurt - as well as further afield to Sydney. Aviation photography is an activity that can easily be fitted into a trip abroad or a family holiday and a few hours spent at a local airport can yield many photos. It's addictive, it's a good way of getting out and about, a good excuse - not that I need one - for travelling and a way to meet new people.

KJ

Years pass, sometimes with unbelievable speed. As with most aspects to life, other things get in the way of what one wants to do and having spent a big chunk of my life doing those other things (one has to earn a living somehow) a remarkable twenty-two years had passed since last using Gatwick as a passenger. A few visits to the observation deck atop the South Terminal, yes at least up until its closure, but not actually flying somewhere - until today. Today, having reinvented myself as an aviation journalist, I am on assignment to spend a day on the Channel Island of Guernsey, reporting on the recently completed redevelopment of the airport.

The trains were on time, and I arrived at Gatwick when I wanted to. Checked in okay, my press photo-card was accepted as good ID. There is something a little surreal about having to provide identification on a flight that is entirely a domestic one, even though, in these now-security conscious days, it has become a necessity – how long before the same is needed for a train ride? Or at any other time?

Having a National UK Press Photo ID card comes in handy sometimes. Actually, very often….I spent some time at the end of the south terminal approach road taking photographs of aircraft on finals – there aren't many but I did see 'my' aircraft arrive. This place doesn't seem anywhere near as busy as it used to be in the days of my forays across the Atlantic with British Caledonian…and they want a second runway? Here? What for?

I took a few shots of the terminal as well, inside and out. No officious officials came barrelling up to question me - sad…I'd have got a kick out of showing them my press card…it works with the police at Heathrow…and for check in…Security no bother, didn't even have to take my shoes off…Looked at the face scanner thingy, no alarms went off, still no officious officials demanding to know things, just sauntered through and followed the sign saying 'To All Departure Gates' and into the shopping mall…

The last time I was here, domestic flights went from the pier to the left of the main building. It had just been demolished (and rebuilding underway) and flights now use all departure gates no matter where they are going. Okay, so everybody has to have ID and everybody is checked so I get that. The main central pier at Gatwick's South Terminal has also been rebuilt – it's not the 'original' original; that was demolished when the present one was built but the second version is actually still there, it's just been buried under multiple add-ons - and as with all flights these days, you get checked again at the gate. Plus, you need your boarding pass so they know where you're going. And if it's an international flight, they won't let you on. So I get that too.

But under the old system, if you were going on a domestic flight, there is no duty-free shopping – obviously – so going into the domestic departure pier was relatively straightforward. Now…the signs saying 'To All Departure gates' takes you winding around through a shopping mall, full of people spending money.

The Channel Islands are treated as domestic destinations so you don't need a passport but Guernsey is not part of the UK and it's not in the EU either, so I 'could' get duty-free goods. The same applies to Jersey and the Isle of Man, and I guess, at a push, *could* also apply to Scotland with the EU referendum, the result of which is endlessly debated, having seen a majority of the Scots vote to remain but the rest of the UK voting to leave the EU…the future remains uncertain. But it's the way that you go around the houses and through all the shops and past sales people wanting to part you from your cash and before you even get to the gate and your waiting aircraft that strikes me. In the old days…I sound so ancient when I say things like that…you went through security and into the departure lounge. The Duty-Free shops were still there but you could bypass them of you wanted to. Now, airside, the entire terminal is one vast mall. Full of shops. And people spending money.

So much for austerity - there ain't much here.

Eventually I found gate 13 (*gate 13…!*) and presented myself, looked in the face recognition thing again, and into the gate lounge. I might have used this gate before…getting on or off a British Caledonian DC10-30 to Dallas. Time was it handled the big long haul jets, now it's a brand spanking new Embraer 195 regional jet of Aurigny Air Services. I haven't been on an E195 before so its something new. And small - I'm used to the idea that an airliner is big and roomy but this is a small jet. Away on time and took some shots out of the aircraft window of the rebuilt Gatwick. One no longer can from the terminal windows – there aren't any.

The morning sun reflects on the English Channel as Hayling Island and the south

UK Wings II

coast passes by and as the land became the sea, it struck me; it was forty-two years ago when I was last on Guernsey, a mere slip of a child on holiday (*forty-two years*…where does the time go? Where do our lives go?), and thus the same decades since I last flew with Aurigny, on the little Islander and Trislander aircraft between Alderney, Jersey *and* Guernsey. It got very cloudy over Cherbourg as we descended but they did look interesting so I photographed them (my dad always did say all I ever did in flight was photograph passing clouds). The ERJ turned to make the final approach over Sark and smoothly touched down on to Guernsey's new runway. This is why I'm here…the rebuilding and levelling of the roller-coaster that aircraft used to land on and take off from. My outstanding memory (and I can still see it as clearly as though it were five minutes ago, even though it was forty-two years) was standing on the roof top viewing deck on the old terminal and watching Viscounts of BEA Channel Islands, British Midland, the yellow-topped Northeast and the orange Cambrian, the Dart Heralds of British Island Airways and the Islanders and Trislanders of Aurigny disappear from sight down the taxiway which dropped markedly as they taxied to the 09 threshold, reappearing at the far end as they reached the runway. This runway had an almost alarming dip in it just past the 09 end and another at the end we're coming in on, 27, approaching from the east. The rebuilding has levelled it considerably but as we turn off, I see the taxiway still has that drop in it so it's down the hill and up the hill to get to the terminal. The runway still undulates a bit too, I notice. Just not as much - nowhere near in fact.

The terminal is new, somewhat anyway, its ten years old now and a much more modern edifice than the one I used a lifetime ago. Sadly however, it does not have an observation deck like the old one. Last off the aircraft – of course – after a chat with the Captain since the E195 is Aurigny's first jet, only three months old and delivered in June, down the steps and on to Guernsian concrete.

I have, once more, left the shores of England and soared through the clouds and across the seas.

Paused to get some shots of the aircraft - nobody seems at all concerned about me hanging about on the ramp taking photos even though I'm not official yet. Into the terminal, through customs - I don't have anything to declare, having ignored the masses demanding money from me for things I don't need in the Gatwick shopping mall. Not that there were any customs officers present - since I was so much later off the aircraft than everybody else, what with chatting up the Captain and loitering on the apron taking photos, the customs people probably thought everybody had come through. Into arrivals and back landside, I'm due to meet the airport's Commercial Manager, Kate Lawson, at 10am so I'm actually early. Took some photos of the inside of the building, went to the airport information desk, and asked the lady there if she could let Kate know I have arrived. Took a seat and waited…a few minutes later I saw a lady come in and go to the info desk.

You know when you're meeting someone how you instinctively know who it is when you see them even though you've never met before? It happened at RAF Brize Norton when I went there for a similar assignment recently, meeting one of their PR people and it was that way now and I stood up to greet Kate as she approached the seating area, my having been pointed out by the very helpful lady behind the info desk. She took me to her car and said it would be easier and quicker to drive round to the admin block rather than walk over and go through all the security gates so out on to a typical Channel Island road…ever see Bergerac on TV do a high-speed chase through roads like this on the other island? Yes. Reality? No chance…not in real life. They don't have wide roads and motorways here. They don't even have cars on Sark (photographed a bit of it as we turned for final approach)…into the admin block, a small building topped by the control tower cab and I'm issued with a pass which gets me anywhere on the airfield, with an escort, but I can otherwise roam. Had a chat with Kate; the airport director, Colin Le Ray, is dealing with a snap CAA inspection so won't be able to see me. I'll email my questions for him to Kate instead. She took me to meet Mark Luty, the Operations Manager, who has a bucket load of photographs and loads them all on to a memory stick so I can take my pick of the ones I want to use for my magazine article.

I was given the grand tour around the airport, riding in a little pick-up truck with 'OPS 1' on the side of it, taking photographs everywhere; the fire station (they even drove the tenders out in front for me to photograph); I went up into the control tower and got some shots from there. I went everywhere actually. Even got a shot of me holding one of my cameras standing on the threshold of runway 09, with the lights on and the tarmac stretching away behind me (it's an 'I-love-me' portrait for my facebook page, taken by ops manager Mark Luty).

It was a fascinating and rewarding day, made even more so by the friendly welcome from a very accommodating airport and its staff. The ride back to Gatwick was on an Aurigny ATR72, another aircraft I haven't been on before so its been an excellent day.

It took more than forty years but when Dad's second wife, my stepmother, Lynda, said all those years ago that a holiday for me would be to get on a plane, go somewhere, ignore the sights and merely look at and photograph the airport, then come home, she was right.

US Airways are now part of aviation history, having merged with American Airlines.

Manchester
2002
(above and below, Kevan James)

MAN remains one of the UK's favourite destinations for the enthusiast, with the aviation viewing park and the top floor of the terminal car park both providing good views.

Manchester's growth over the past decade has been remarkable, bringing worldwide air travel within reach of a sizeable part of the northwest of England. The airport is also redeveloping its terminals to cater for the continuing expansion of services.
(Tyler McDowell)

Guernsey

The Channel Island of Guernsey has a small but comfortable and efficient airport that is easy to use. The primary airlines are Aurigny and Blue Islands. The airport is also served by Flybe and in the summer, other UK airlines as well as those from Europe.
Main image - Aurigny Trislander G-JOEY served Aurigny and the Channel Islands for over 40 years and was an iconic symbol of inter-island travel.
(all images Kevan James)

(all images Kevan James)

A quiet evening ride.... **GCI-LGW**

Manchester is unique among UK airports with the viewing park situated next to the taxiway and within easy sight of the runway, providing up close and personal looks at what passes by. The airport also has a good viewpoint on the top of the car park behind the terminals which allows a slightly distant but good view of the ramp areas in front of it and an excellent view of aircraft parked at the terminal to the right. Top four images taken from the viewing park. Main image - there are two raised mounds that give excellent views across the runways and towards the terminals *(all images Tyler McDowell)*

Boeing 777, Manchester (Tyler McDowell)

Belfast Aldergrove

Belfast's Aldergrove served as the primary gateway to Northern Ireland for years before much of the regular traffic moved to the re-opened Belfast City. BFS is still a busy place however, with many of the movements low-fare airlines. *(all images Tyler McDowell)*

BFS

Belfast City

Named after one of the city's most famous sons, footballer George Best, the airport is well located and handles most of the scheduled legacy airline traffic. Top two - on one side is the Harland and Wolff shipbuilding yards and the plant of Bombardier. On the other is the district of Sydenham - centre left - from which the airport took its original name.
(all images Tyler McDowell)

TMcD

There are some airports around the world that, for any airline aficionado, have to be visited, even if only once. Heathrow is the obvious one for UK residents despite not having any on-airport viewing facilities, closely followed by Manchester which does. Zurich is another, although Switzerland may not the cheapest country to visit so a little closer to the UK is Frankfurt, well known for the welcome given to spotters and photographers, as is Düsseldorf; most German airports have somewhere decent to watch the comings and goings.

But there is one in Europe that stands out and for a geographically small country that has just one major international airport and a airline that, in terms of size, seems out of all proportion to the country it serves, it is a remarkable place. Home to the national airline of the Netherlands, KLM Royal Dutch Airlines, Amsterdam Schipol Airport (AMS) was also where the Fokker Aircraft Company built the F27, F28 and F100 airliners. The Dutch are also very friendly, English is spoken by almost everybody and so attractive is it – and so easy to get to - I have visited Amsterdam four times recently.

The word 'Schipol' means 'Ships Hole' and going back in history far enough, the area was once notorious for the number of ships that sank there, hence the name. The Dutch are an innovative people and drained what was once the Harlem Lake and filled it, creating an expanse of flat land, part of which is now occupied by the country's primary airport. As land that was once covered by the sea, in a country that has always been very low level, AMS is the only airport in the world where the altimeter in an aircraft cockpit tells its pilot that they are now thirteen feet *below* sea level when on the ground. The airport is a hot spot for European aviation enthusiasts and also attracts people from all over the world, standing equally with London Heathrow, Paris, Frankfurt and Zurich as one of Europe's busiest airports.

Amsterdam has direct flights to almost every airport in the United Kingdom, operated by multiple airlines, most obviously British Airways and KLM, with Flybe and easyJet also prominent; British Airways even has a Boeing 767-300 operating a peak-time morning LHR service among its many Airbus A320 services to Heathrow & Gatwick as well as extra BA Cityflyer operations to London City (LCY) and a new Vueling Airlines service to Luton, competing directly with easyJet. From the four London airports alone, the International Airlines Group (IAG), the parent company of British Airways and Vueling, have some 18 daily flights to Amsterdam.

Whilst Amsterdam has many off-airport spotting points, a lot of which provide excellent shots of aircraft taxiing or taking off and landing without fences in the way since AMS employ the simple yet effective security measure of deep ditches around the airport, I have always used the famous (and aptly named) Panorama Terrace, otherwise known in days gone by as the observation deck. The terrace is accessible from the landside area; you can get to it by going to the KLM Check-in desks where signage directs you to a staircase that takes the visitor up two flights to the Dakota Bar and Touchdown restaurant and entry to the Viewing Platform is free (as of my last visit in November 2016). A preserved Fokker F100 of KLM Cityhopper wearing the registration PH-OFE resides on the deck and which is also free for a look inside (Sister-ship PH-OFA is at the Aviodrome in Lyelstad). The Panorama Terrace is open from 7am to 9pm in the summer season and 9am to 7pm in the winter season

AMS has what is essentially one massive terminal but is divided in two, in between which is a huge shopping centre. From the day the building opened in the mid-1960s, AMS has always made shopping an integral part of the terminal and even more so today. The shopping area is landside and also acts as a central area for people to start their journeys into the Netherlands, with access to the train station, buses and taxis. Near the middle of it all is a small aviation hobby and toy shop that has parts of aircraft preserved for people to admire and explore with a Douglas DC-9 fuselage and cockpit section and the central wheel bogie and engine of a Douglas DC-10 on display.

On one occasion I stayed in the Terminal overnight - a place that usually has thousands filling it by day seemed almost other-worldly with only a handful of people waiting for the next day to arrive. The empty desks and lack of airline personnel around also made it easy for some unusual photographs.

Airside at Amsterdam Schipol, you can get decent shots of aircraft from most of the gates, although shooting through the windows can be a problem. The D-Gates (which most KLM, CityJet and BA flights depart from) can also provide excellent shots of taxiing aircraft. Although it's not a long distance from London, the presence of the north sea between the UK and Holland makes flying quicker than a boat trip and since my first visit in 2015 I have flown with KLM on one of their Boeing 737-700 aircraft, twice on CityJet's Avro RJ85 and two KLM Cityhopper Fokker F70s.

I also travelled with one of the more exotic airlines that flew between London and Amsterdam; Indonesian carrier Garuda. With Fifth-Freedom rights on the route, I booked a cheap deal (£39) from Gatwick, although one way, so looked up flights back to Gatwick or City Airport and found CityJet offering one-way for only £41 at the time, given my previous flight with them, I knew it was a good deal to spend that and get everything included instead of paying £35 for a low fare airline (the cheapest at the time) yet have to pay for everything else. Outbound, I got on Garuda's Boeing 777-300(ER) at LGW a good 30 minutes before we were due to depart. I am used to flying on narrow-bodies so getting on a Boeing 777 for such a short flight was a little different. Unfortunately this service would be terminating five weeks later as Garuda were to move its Jakarta to London service to Heathrow, with AMS served separately. The flight took about 10 minutes to taxi to the runway and we left on time. After we began to cruise on our flight, a snack box was served along with a bottle of water. Not a lot of choice compared to KLM, but for a very short flight it wasn't bad, containing a Vegetarian Wrap (Tomato Puree, Mushroom and Cheese) and a Coconut/Raspberry cake.

We began to descend towards AMS whilst still over the North Sea. We had only been at our cruising altitude for around 10 minutes, reflecting the short flight time. Touchdown was a good ten minutes ahead of schedule, however a lengthy taxi took up the time as we had to get to the Terminal building from the runway but it did leave me with a full day at AMS, Schipol deservedly being of Europe's hotspots for the commercial aviation enthusiast.

Amsterdam is deservedly one of Europe's top aviation attractions, the famous Panorama Terrace giving good views over the central ramp area. Views and photography from inside the terminal are also good, although care needs to be taken when shooting through the windows.
(all images Tyler McDowell)

(all images Tyler McDowell)

Netherlands
AMS
Schipol
Amsterdam

Schipol
Amsterdam
AMS

Like most major airports, AMS bustles by day and gets very quiet at night. Life in the control tower is however, a twenty-four hour a day operation.
(all images Tyler McDowell)

Airport Days and Nights Terminals and Runways

TMcD

Most people tend to think of airlines as companies that transport people but at one time, aviation thinking held that the future for air transport was cargo rather than passengers. From its earliest days, air mail has always been one of the principal reasons for using aircraft (ask yourself how a letter posted in Brighton, on England's south coast, can be delivered to an address in Thurso in Scotland, the northernmost town on mainland UK, or for that matter the Shetland islands even further north, the next day) and early airport planning included large cargo terminals.

Since those days, the increased size of airliners enabled most cargo to be put in the baggage hold of the aircraft since passenger's bags, even on a full flight, actually take up little of the enormous space under the cabin of the average airliner. Even so, dedicated Cargo aircraft are numerous and even passenger aircraft don't have room for large bulky items. Since many of them fly at night, cargo hauling aircraft are not often seen during the day except parked in the distance, apparently not doing very much, sometimes on a hard-to-see ramp. There are however, a number of airports that, although having been less used for passenger flights, have had the available space taken up by all-cargo airlines and become hubs for such operations. One of them is Germany's Cologne/Bonn

Cologne/Bonn (CGN) has become one of the best airports to go to in Europe for Cargo carriers and I have it on good authority from local enthusiasts that Sunday is the best day for these flights, but I am yet to visit on a Sunday. However my visits to the Airport in August 2015 & April 2016 left a good impression of the airport on me. Its 1970 terminal with two satellites attached to it and designed to have two more when expansion was needed, has instead been joined by a second passenger building compete with the now obligatory shopping area and on its original terminal, a viewing deck overlooks both terminals and directly in front of it, stretching into the distance, the Cargo ramp. CGN is home to low-fare airline, Germanwings, who now make up a sizeable number of flights and the airport also sees regular Air Berlin & TUIfly traffic. There is also an increasing presence of other low-fare airlines establishing themselves at Cologne, Ryanair, Norwegian and Wizzair being three. Other international traffic and scheduled carriers include Austrian Airlines, Turkish Airlines, Iran Air and Blue Air. Some major international names have left Cologne in recent times, most due to the recession years (2008-2014) causing a fall in demand as well as increased competition from the newer carriers at the airport. These include KLM Cityhopper (Amsterdam Schipol) a service which has operated on and off for decades, Continental Airlines (New York/Newark) and easyJet (London Gatwick). Part of the reason is also the close proximity of Dusseldorf, with the legacy carriers being more certain of filling seats with flights from there instead of CGN.

United Postal Service (UPS) is the most prominent Cargo Airline at CGN, the airline's dedicated cargo handling buildings occupying a sizable portion of the airport's central area with a mixture of Boeing 747-400(F), Boeing 757-200(F), Boeing 767-300(WL/F) and McDonnell-Douglas MD-11F operating its flights. Federal Express, or FedEx as it is more often known, has a daily service to Memphis using a Boeing 777-200(F) and some smaller feeder services using various equipment including Boeing 757-200(F), McDonnell-Douglas MD-11 and even an ATR-42 on lease from ASL Ireland. DHL, Egyptair Cargo, Bluebird Cargo and Star Air (amongst others) make up the rest of the Cargo Hub.

For spotting and photography at Cologne/Bonn I have used the Viewing Deck but also taken a number of shots from inside both Terminals. On three of my four flights using Cologne/Bonn (two flights in, two flights out) I have shot pictures from the ramp as well since Ryanair do not use enclosed air bridges. Outside Terminal 2 sits a unique and now permanent resident in the Car Park - the Zero-Gravity Airbus A300 (F-BAUD) that was replaced by a younger ex-Luftwaffe Airbus A310. The aircraft was retired in 2013 and during 2014 was placed at its new location for generations of travellers throughout Europe to observe when they come to Cologne.

Terminal 2 is the more modern of the two passenger buildings, where all the airlines not associated with Lufthansa or Star Alliance operate from. The southeastern glass end wall of Terminal 2 also provides a good view towards the threshold of the airport's primary runway, at 3,800m, its longest and aircraft can be seen easily taxiing to and from T2's gates.

For any spotter in Europe, Cologne/Bonn makes a good day out or even a decent overnight trip as there are a handful of local hotels and motels offering cheap nights from around £40 a person.

∎

Cologne/Bonn
Germany

Cologne/Bonn's rooftop Besucher Terrasse offers excellent views of much of Terminal 1's ramp and a decent look at aircraft taxiing to and from Terminal 2. Landing shots when runway 14 is in use are excellent and an early start provides the opportunity for some ethereal images of the sunrise over the airport *(all images Tyler McDowell)*

CGN Germany Cologne / Bonn

Opened in March 1970, CGN's Terminal 1 is very different from the more modern T2 and its glass-box shape. T1 retains a more individual look, the observation terrace and displays of the airport's history. Main image - gate C1 was used by Pan Am on the run to West Berlin in the 1970s.
(all images Tyler McDowell)

9
Globetrotting

You are never too old to set another goal or dream a new dream

C. S. Lewis

FJ
One of my favourite countries to visit is Australia, with its largely pleasant climate, friendly people, interesting wildlife and stunning night skies. I have made four visits to Australia over the years, going by various routes. This time, I visited for a couple of weeks between 29th March and 12th April 2016, at the start of the Southern autumn, when the weather was still warm and sunny. During my Australia trips over the years I've found the weather in the Southern Hemisphere can be just as bad as the UK at times, particularly in autumn and winter, despite what the media, Aussie soap operas and glossy websites would have you believe, but this time I was fortunate in that the only rain I saw was showers on my first day and some heavier rain on my last morning there as I was waiting for my flight home. That said, the climate there is less unpredictable and changeable than the UK climate - believe it or not Sydney actually gets more rain than London but it does have fewer days on which that rain falls. My visit was not primarily for aviation photography and I only had a few days either side of a trip out to the west of the Great Dividing Range but I still managed to get plenty of photos so, even if you do have limited time, it is well worth a visit.

Sydney Airport, which is 8km south of the city centre, is Australia's busiest, handling over 35,600,000 passengers in 2011 and 326,686 aircraft movements in 2013. It offers not just a good variety of aircraft and airlines - including international flights to Asia, other Oceania destinations and the USA and onwards to Europe as well as regional services within Australia - but also good opportunities for photography and spotting.

Due to its somewhat isolated location to the south east of Asia, Australia with its population of around 23 million people is dependent on aviation and this is reflected in the variety of aircraft and airlines you see at Sydney and the other major airports. The fact that the country is so vast means that aircraft are an essential way of getting around domestically as well and there are plenty of regional services. Sydney is a hub for Qantas, Virgin Australia and Jetstar - as you'd expect, they make up the majority of the traffic on view - and is visited by most major international airlines, including British Airways, American Airlines, ANA and Emirates, among many others, along more exotic airlines such as Aircalin, Fiji Airways and Cebu (from the Philippines). Cargo airlines are also well-represented by the likes of UPS and FedEx with their MD-11s and Polar Air Cargo. Aircraft types on view vary from the huge A380 and 747 right down to tiny Saabs employed on regional services and also business jets. You can on occasion see government aircraft, including an Royal Australian Air Force 737 which took Australian Prime Minister Malcolm Turnbull from Sydney down to Canberra one afternoon when I was there.

Sydney has three runways 16R/34L ('north-south'), 16L/34R ('third') and 07/25 ('east-west') which crosses 16R/34L. However, due to noise abatement regulations, as the airport is surrounded by residential areas except Botany Bay to the south, there is a curfew between 2300 and 0600 and during the day airport operations are restricted to 80 movements per hour at peak times. The good thing about the night curfew from a spotting perspective is that you don't miss anything since nothing will

Globetrotting

be arriving or leaving in the dead of night.

The journey didn't start well when I looked out of my hotel window at Heathrow to see the Singapore Airlines A380 I was supposed to fly on abort its landing and head straight back into the clouds. There was a violent storm raging with gusts of nearly 100mph meaning there was a fair bit of disruption at Heathrow and other southern airports; I got to the desk at the terminal to be told what no traveller wants to hear: 'Your flight is delayed as the plane has been diverted to Manchester because of the storms'. That wasn't great, especially as it would seriously mess with my schedule, but I discovered that an earlier Singapore Airlines flight had made it in and was scheduled to depart half an hour late, so I asked if there was any chance I could get on that one. As it happened there were spare seats and I escaped Heathrow and the storm mayhem aboard a lovely Boeing 777-300ER (9V-SWP). It was a good flight and, like a lot of people, I used the time to catch up on films I hadn't seen, such as Star Wars: The Force Awakens.

On landing in Singapore, I had a walk round the terminal which has good views of aircraft at the gates. I didn't have long in Singapore and it was soon time to go through security - which, instead of a central security point in places such as LHR, and other western airports - is located at the gate. Once I got to the desk though, I was told by a young woman with a severe manner that because I had changed my flight - despite the fact it was Singapore Airlines who agreed quite happily to change it for me - it would have repercussions for my flight back home in a couple of weeks. I dismissed that as nonsense as it was not a round-the-world trip, just an out-and-back to Australia, and it turned out that I was right and the prophet of doom at the desk was wrong although it was a pity I couldn't let her know that.

My next flight, an 8-hour daytime flight to Sydney, was also on a Boeing 777-300ER, this time painted in the all-white Star Alliance scheme, registered 9V-SWI. Normally all-white is boring but this looked quite attractive. Sadly I was so tired by this point, that the flight mostly passed me by, apart from the occasional sleepy look at the real-time map showing our position on the IFE system. I was properly woken up on landing in Sydney by the thrust reversers, which were incredibly loud. Once in the terminal, immigration was simple; as a UK passport-holder I could, along with a few other nationalities, use the self-service passport control which took less than a minute and far quicker than queueing to go through the took less than a minute and far quicker than queueing to go through the manned desks. However, on reaching the baggage carousel it eventually became apparent that my bag hadn't been as fortunate as me. It was still in Singapore, having left London many hours behind me! I provided my details, was given $150 in compensation and some 'essentials' and went to find my hotel which was literally just across the road from the terminal. This is the famous Rydges Sydney Airport Hotel which is not only convenient for the airport but good for watching aircraft activity, too. On my first day my grand plans to get out and about went completely out of the window when I didn't wake up until 1.48pm, thanks to the long flights, jet lag, and the inconvenience of having to find out where my bag had got to, so I decided to go no further than the viewing deck of Rydges Hotel where I was staying. The Rydges viewing area, which is accessed via the aptly-named 'Dreamliner Lounge', affords great views over the terminals towards the city centre. However, even for hotel guests, it is not free to visit and costs $10 to use (although that $10 does include a free drink, including alcoholic beverages) and access is also dependent on whether the hotel is hosting a function.

Should you not be able to access the viewing deck at the hotel, for whatever reason, then the multi-storey car park next door is just as good if not better - take the lift up to the 8th floor to get you above obstructions such as buildings and light poles. The Rydges viewing area and the next-door car park both have great views of the aprons at the International and Domestic terminals as well as aircraft approaching on runway 16R (in which case you can get great shots of them with the Sydney skyline in the background) or departing on 34L. I spent a couple of happy hours up on the viewing deck, dodging the light rain showers, before going back inside, where I discovered that reception had my bag after its delayed journey from London. The following morning I got a taxi from the hotel to a well-known local spotting location known as the Tower Mound, so named due to its location next to the control tower. It's also known as 'Shep's Mound' after a local spotter who passed away in 2005 and is a piece of public land just off of General Holmes Drive, and handily placed for a McDonald's and a BP service station (or 'servo') just a short walk away; when you want to head back to your hotel or the airport itself, just phone for a cab. The one downside of this location is that, despite the elevated mound, the view is quite restricted by ongoing (at the time of writing in 2016) construction works to put a double fence in, so there is construction equipment, temporary lighting poles and portacabins in the way. Also, photos of aircraft across the airfield are affected by heat haze although, by mid-morning when haze starts to really become a nuisance, the sun is getting far enough round that you'd be considering re-locating to another place anyway.

Because of the heat by then, it's time to go and do something else for a few hours until later in the afternoon. Take a hat, water and sunscreen as well, because there's no shade at the spot although, as already mentioned, McDonalds and the BP servo, with its shop, are not far away. On my first visit I didn't have any of these things, instead using my hoodie as makeshift sun protection although by the time things got uncomfortable, the heat and the haze was starting to get bad and it was time to leave anyway. From mid-afternoon, the best spot is 'the Beach', or to give it its correct name, Kyeemagh Beach, which has a car park next to the airport's old control tower. Here you can see and photograph everything which is taking off from 16R or landing on 34L or taxiing to or from the terminals depending in the direction of take-off or landing. However, on a full frame camera you might want something longer than 300mm for anything other than side on shots of large airliners; a large zoom such as an 80-400mm (the Canon equivalent is 100-400mm) or 200-500 would be ideal - Canon don't have an equivalent of Nikon's 200-500 but there are reasonable third party 150-600mm zoom lenses available, made by Sigma and Tamron.

This was by far my favourite spot and, as someone with a soft spot for all things that float as well, it was nice to photograph planes with the container ships at Port Botany in the background. This is a popular spot, not just with spotters and photographers, but with locals for walking their dogs - and horses - and fishing. You can get some interesting photos of aircraft on the runway with people, dogs and horses in the foreground and container ships in the background. These were the locations I visited most often in the few days I had available but I also went to one place near the container port at Botany Bay, a location called Millstream Lookout.

You can get great shots of aircraft arriving and departing on the third runway but the downside of this spot is the fact you need a car to get there, although I was lucky and got rides from Australian friends, which saved me the expense of hiring one. There are no facilities, although there are public toilets just down the road at the boat ramp, towards Port Botany. You do not need a long lens here, 200mm is ideal. After my trip west of the mountains, to rural New South Wales, I had another couple of days for photography and spent it in the same locations as before.

All too soon though, it was time to leave Australia and fly back home to the UK, again via Singapore. In contrast to the Boeing 777-300s I had on the way out, I had Airbus A380s on the way home, both of which were full. I was in an aisle seat but could easily see out of the window over the wing and you can really appreciate the colossal wing span of these things; it is a huge aircraft. It's also pretty noisy as the engines are quite quiet which makes the sound of the hydraulics more pronounced and there were plenty of whines, whirrs, thuds, groans and bangs. It was easy to hear the flaps moving and the main landing gear being stowed and un-stowed during take-off and landing; 20 wheels make quite a noise and a few small children started to cry at the unanticipated assault on their young ears.

We landed on time at Heathrow and it wasn't long before I was off the plane and out of the terminal into a chilly April morning but it would have been quicker if a bunch of schoolchildren returning from a trip hadn't been in front of me and one hadn't had a damaged passport…

Sydney is well worth a visit for the 'spotter' and photographer with its variety of aircraft, airlines and places to watch the action. It's ideal for a hard-core spotting and photography trip in itself or for a day or two as part of a longer general trip. There are airlines not seen in Europe, mainly benign weather and plenty of opportunities for photos with interesting backgrounds, whether it's the city skyline or the container port behind your planes. The only disappointment, for want of a better word, was that I had heard that the All Nippon Airways (ANA) Boeing 787 which carries the depiction of Star Wars droid R2D2 was a regular visitor but there wasn't a sign of it when I was there, which sums up my complete non-luck with special schemes. There isn't a large aviation enthusiast community in Australia, it isn't the same as the UK or the rest of Europe, or even parts of the US due mainly to a smaller population but the scene, certainly around Sydney, is active and friendly, at least from my experience. If you are a traveller visiting Australia for the first time, don't be afraid to ask for help. Aussies are generally a friendly bunch of people. I had no problems with public transport or getting a taxi although I am lucky and know a few people there so I managed to score a lot of lifts.

I'll definitely be heading back for more photography and spotting in the not too distant future.

∎

SYDNEY
Australia

Image courtesy of Sydney Airport

SYDNEY
AUSTRALIA

To find airlines that are not seen in Europe means travelling to somewhere that is not in Europe...Sydney being as good a place as any; carefully picking their way around Shep's Mound, one of the airport's favoured spotting areas, are Exotica Pacifica - Air Vanuatu, Fiji Airways and Tigerair. Bottom right - one airline that is seen worldwide is the fast-growing LAN Chile, crossing the Pacific from South America with thier brand new Boeing 787s. Main image - Cebu Pacific from the Philippines *(all images Fay Johnson)*

Virgin Australia Airbus A330
Sydney *(Fay Johnson)*

Berlin Tegel

(all images Tyler McDowell)

Above, right and centre - Berlin Tegel's open air viewing deck is good for getting up close and personal. Main image - the old 1970s terminal was on the other side of the runways

TXL Berlin Tegel

Right - one of the airlines not seen too much in the west is Mongolian but even they now operate western aircraft. Below and right - Tegel's terminal roof-top viewing deck means a good look at almost everything. *(Tyler Mc Dowell)*

Left - partners to prosperity. Main image - one of the more eye-catching colour schemes to emerge from the east, S7 Airlines. *(Tyler McDowell)*

FRA Germany Frankfurt

Top left - Even in the rain, a brand new Airbus A350 looks sleek, clean and fresh. Top right - Istanbul Airlines bring a splash of colour. Above left - Lufthansa remain one of the few users of the MD11 Cargo hauler. Above right - at night, the cargo ramps come alive *(top four images Fay Johnson).* Main image - Fra's main parallel runways, terminals on the right and in the distance the newest runway, the airport's fourth. The crosswind runway runs from the far end of the two main runways and off to the left. Centre left is the site of the former US Air Base, soon to be Frankfurt's newest terminal. *(Stefan Rebscher/Fraport AG)*

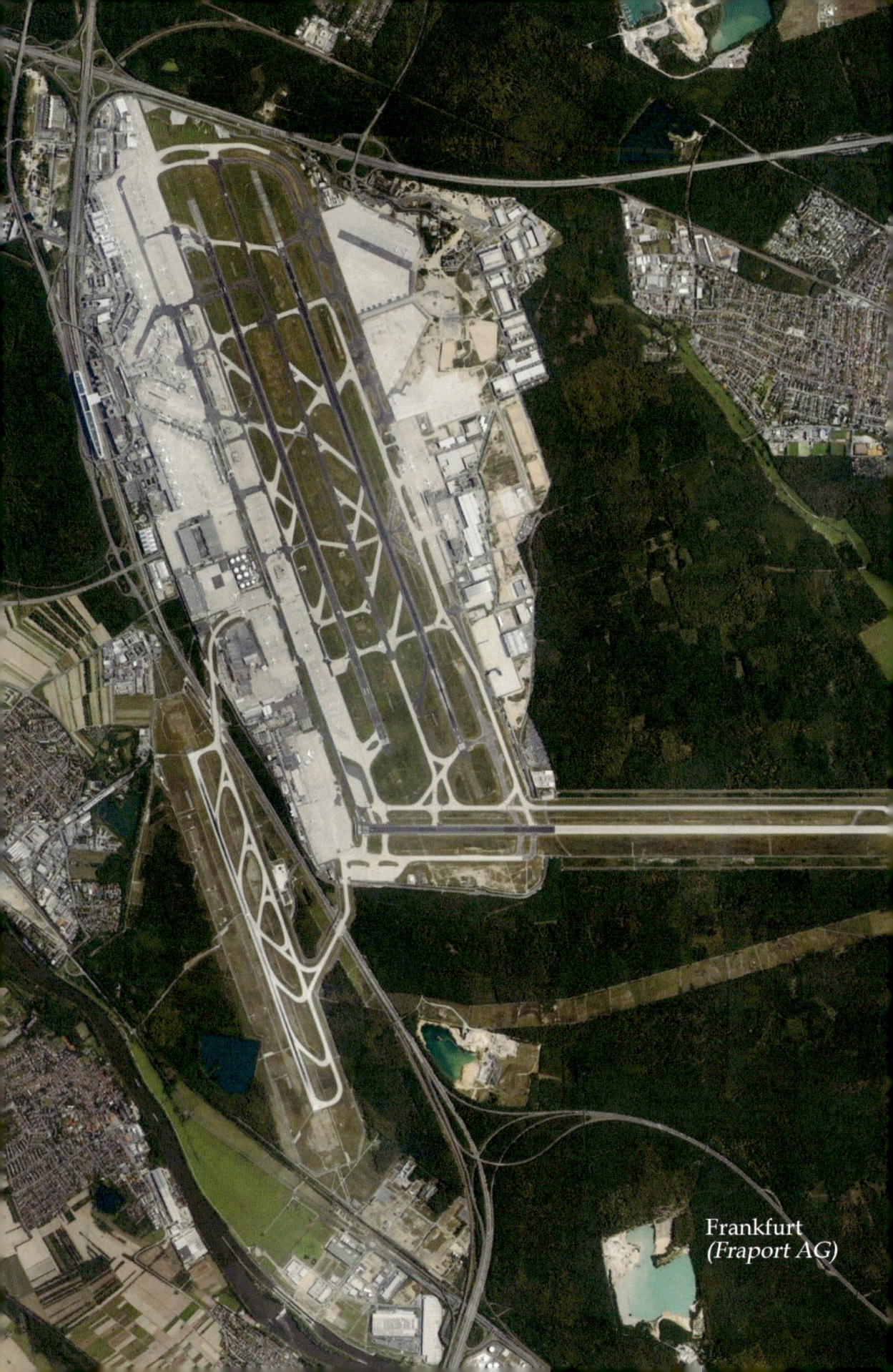

Frankfurt
(Fraport AG)

All airports can be somewhat ghostly at night and Helsinki is no exception. But when the sun rises and the mists of the dark begin to clear, the roads and the runways begin to get busy. Operated by the appropriately named Finavia, HEL's movements are overseen by the stylish control tower.
(all images Tyler McDowell)

HEL
Helsinki FINLAND

FINLAND
HELSINKI

Above and left -
Helsinki has a good spread of airline service although unsurprisingly given the close proximity to Russia, Aeroflot figure quite strongly.
Below left - despite the Flybe titles, the ATR is registered in Finland.
Main image - Helsinki's golden sunrise.
(all images Tyler McDowell)

Los Angeles LAX California

City of Angels

Los Angeles, California - Despite the modernity of the Tom Bradley International Terminal - left - extended to handle the A380, the original satellites - top left and right - are still in use, the oval shape apparent. Each one was first reached by underground passages but now are accessed above ground with additional gates added.

Main image - LAX's Tom Bradley International terminal, centre and American and Delta's terminals nearest the camera *(all images Pablo Herrera)*

Los Angeles
California

Theme Building and control tower (Pablo Herrera)

Los Angeles remains one of the world's busiest airports. With Hollywood on its doorstep, its not uncommon to see film crews at work and movie stars coming and going. Unsurprisingly the Airbus A380 is seen frequently with Australian airline QANTAS having up to four on the ground at LAX at the same time

California
USA LAX

(all images Fay Johnson)

MIA Florida
the sunshine state

Miami, Florida
Although Miami retains the shape of the original terminal, and the hotel towering above it, internally it has been modernised, with gate concourses rebuilt completely. The result is an up-to-date and comfortable International Airport *(all images Pablo Herrera)*

Florida MIAMI

A favourite place at Miami for catching landing aircraft with a camera is the southern perimeter. Left - Eastern reborn; over two decades after the original airline left the skies a new carrier using the name was born. Below left and right - Cargo has always been an important part of Miami's operations. Amerijet still fly the 727 and Cargolux the latest Boeing 747-800. Main image - Florida's golden sunset.

(all images Pablo Herrera)

Switzerland
Zurich

(all images Tyler McDowell)

ZRH Zurich

The unusual becomes the usual at ZRH....
Previous page - no words needed.
This page -
below; the famous apron tour bus and ZRH's famous observation deck make the Swiss city one of the 'must-visit' airports for the enthusiast.
(all images Tyler McDowell)

Zurich Kloten ZRH Switzerland

Switzerland is one of the world's most beautiful countries and ZRH one of the most scenic locations.
(all images Flughafen Zurich AG)

Montevideo
(Pablo Herrera)

10
Conversation

I don't see why in 10 years' time you wouldn't fly people for free. Why don't airports pay us for delivering the passengers to their shops?

Ryanair CEO Michael O'Leary (on low fares)

KJ & PH

Like me, Pablo Herrera is a journalist. Unlike me, he covers more mainstream news, while I tend to be more limited to matters of an aeronautical nature (although not exclusively). We all have our specialties but both Pablo and I share an interest in Aviation so it seemed logical for us to talk, especially since his travels have covered much of South America

'I don't know where my aviation passion came from, it's always been there – it just is,' I said. 'It's been there for most of my life so how did your interest in aviation begin?' I asked.

'I grew up in Caracas, Venezuela,' Pablo replied. 'During my childhood and early teenage years my family's apartment was facing the runway of an airport that was nestled in the middle of the Eastern part of the city. Popularly known as La Carlota (Officially Base Aérea Generalísimo Francisco de Miranda), it served Government, Military and General Aviation. The traffic there was impressive. On weekdays it was mostly business jets (including the US Embassy Gulfstream) and Government aircraft (including the Venezuelan 'Air Force One', first a Hawker Siddeley 748, then a Boeing 737-200), as well as military transport classics like the DC-3. Also, plenty of military helicopters and the so called 'Tango-Tango-Fox', a Cessna 150E, offering the first service of a radio station (Radio Caracas Televisión) with live traffic reports from the air.

'My school was situated just under the landing path, around 700 meters away from the runway, so all the planes constantly flew over me while on finals. Then, on weekends, it was a festival. Friday evenings and Saturday mornings was the time when private aircraft would take off full of families going to many tourist destinations around the country (most notably the paradisiac islands of Los Roques). Sunday late afternoon was the real rush time, when all of them came back practically at the same time. I would listen to ATC on my FM radio, take note of every aircraft's registration, looked for them up in the air with my binoculars while circling the city on hold and keep a record of the most active ones. In a time when there was no Internet, no Google, I managed to learn everything about the beauties that populated that airport; Cessnas, Beechcrafts, Pipers… It was the golden age of Venezuela and so it reflected in how many people owned their private planes for leisure. The airport wouldn't normally operate at night, so the runway was at dark, no lights on ever. But…only on very special occasions they used it, especially for emergency situations or government requirements. When it happened, it was the cherry on top of the cake. I was like living inside the runway. I was mesmerized by the spectacle in front of me.

'Occasionally, the airport organized air shows, which I would eagerly attend in order to have a close contact with the airport and spot my apartment from the tarmac. I barely remember my first two flights, as I moved with my family from Barcelona, Spain, to Caracas, Venezuela. I was only four at the time. But then, at nine, came my real first crush with Commercial Aviation. After all my learning and plane sightings from my balcony I had the chance to feel like being part of the show I was witnessing. I went with my family on a vacation to Mexico and Florida.

Conversation

'Flying those DC-8's and a DC-9 on that occasion confirmed to me that I was in love with this thing called Aviation. I was so impressed with the wide variety of airlines, colours and aircraft I saw at Miami in 1971, that I decided at that time that Commercial Aviation was the sexiest thing ever. Shortly after that trip I started drawing my routes on a map I got from a Geography book. On a side note, La Carlota airport was closed to GA traffic in the 90's, since it was too crowded and was becoming dangerous for the city because of the heavy traffic. Currently it's only used by the Government and there a plans to close it permanently and build a city park there'.

I nodded. It's not an unfamiliar tale. 'You're a journalist; who do you work for, what do you cover? Any specialities?' I asked.

'I am a Foreign Affairs correspondent. I've been doing this since 1990, although I started working as a Sports commentator for a radio station in 1984 in the city where I was born (Barcelona, Spain), where I was attending Journalism School. Doing Sports for the first 4 years of my career allowed me to do my first travels as a professional, which quickly got me engaged to this. I covered some UEFA football games, motorcycling competitions, basketball games, cycling courses and, top of the cake, the 1988 Olympics (both Winter in Calgary and Summer in Seoul).

'I was hired by El Periódico de Catalunya, the most popular newspaper in Barcelona at the time, to join the Sports team, but I quickly expressed to my editor how interested I actually was in joining the Foreign Affairs department. I was lucky enough to start my new duties when the Eastern European countries were asking for the end of Communism, so just a few days later I was on my way to Sofia to cover the elections in Bulgaria. That summer of 1990, Saddam Hussein's Iraq invaded Kuwait. Most of my colleagues were vacationing and, since I was the newest and the youngest, they offered me the chance to go and cover the Operation Desert Shield/Desert Storm events in the Gulf.

'That kind of made me look to my bosses as an intrepid young guy willing to be the next War Correspondent. So from then on I got to cover most of the wars and conflicts going during the 1990s'.

It rather reminds me of my father; he spent his career working for the British Forces Broadcasting Service (BFBS) and it meant being wherever the UK's Armed Forces were, including combat zones. I was born in Cyprus when the ENOSIS struggles were at their height. Bombs went off all the time and Dad had to carry a gun. He spent a period in Aden when a similar independence conflict there was at its peak – families weren't sent though, it was too dangerous so I remained in London. BFBS were in the Falklands, Iraq and Afghanistan as well, although Dad had retired by then.

'Did you ever get shot at?' I asked curiously.

'Well, I've been through a few scary instances of being caught in the middle of a shoot-out, or a bombing, or even sniper fire. But none of those were directly targeted to me. I was not that important, I guess,' Pablo laughed quietly.

'Honestly, I never feared for my life being at any of those dangerous places, although I once went through a really high risk of being kidnapped, and a couple of times I was in the middle of a mob with very angry people yelling at me. But all went good at the end'. He smiled.

'So having survived, what next?'

'In 2000, I was hired by CNN to join the newly created Spanish language unit, so I moved to Atlanta. For the first five years I was at the Newsroom as a copy editor. Then, one day, I decided I wanted to be on the field again, and try reporting, instead of with a notebook, with a camera. I became a freelance, purchased my own technical equipment and off I went. Internet flight booking was beginning to boom at the time, along with the low cost carriers. So suddenly I saw myself immersed in my own dream'. He smiled again.

'I could pick the places where I wanted to go to cover certain topics for the TV, and, best of all, I could pick what route to take, what airline, what detour, what airport…' Pablo's smile grew wider. 'Eventually I started working for other media, so I could multiply my chances and combine my work with my passion. My period working as an International correspondent allowed me to fly to places you would never think of going at all during a lifetime. Also, I got the chance to fly many military and official aircraft, to places that are not your usual airport.

'Since I was about 11 years old, after a trip from Venezuela to the US on vacation, I've always been obsessed with trying different routes and populate my route map with as many different lines from point A to point B as possible. I felt kind of frustrated every time I was repeating a route, or if I had to go back to my home city by the same way. That's why when I book a trip, I always try to get an intermediate stop on the way back, especially if it's a new one.

'Let's say, if I fly LHR-JFK, on my way back I would try doing JFK-BOS-LHR; or even JFK-CDG-LHR. That way, I got to add more flights, add more hours, more airports, maybe airlines…'

'I know the feeling,' I said. 'Many of my flights have been on the same routes, London to Cyprus and Dallas in the US. It would be nice to vary things more.'

Pablo nodded. 'Currently, I'm based in Miami, working as a freelance News writer for the Telemundo network. My duties don't involve too much travelling (I think I needed a break after 25 years), but being a freelance gives me plenty of time now to do plane spotting trips'.

'So how much of Central and South America have you seen and flown to?' I asked - time to cut to the chase and talk about airports.

'I've been to all countries in Central America except for one, Belize, which I intend it to visit rather soon. Of all of them, only in one, Honduras, I haven't been to the capital (Tegucigalpa's Toncontín), only to San Pedro Sula. In South America I still have a few missing, like Bolivia, Perú and Argentina. I've always wanted to circle the globe over the Southern Hemisphere, so my next adventure will most likely start in Sao Paulo and finish in Santiago, Chile, or Buenos Aires, after flying to South Africa, Australia and New Zealand. I have logged a few very interesting and not too visited ones, like Carrasco at Montevideo in Uruguay, Palmira, Colombia, which serves Cali and its surrounding region, Asuncion, Guarani in Paraguay, Guayaquil or Quito, as well as a good quantity of them in Venezuela, the country where I grew up. I'm very proud of having been to all of those, especially Carrasco, which is the southernmost capital city in the Americas'.

'So which is the busiest South American airport?' I asked, never having had the pleasure of going to South America or for that matter Central America either.

'Sao Paulo happens to be that one, which is also my favourite in the region because of the variety of international carriers and the great amount of domestic and regional traffic within the Americas, with all kinds of aircraft, from wide bodies to regional jets and even props. It's a bustling place inside the terminal and even without leaving it, let's say, if you're on a layover, you can feel and sense the Brazilian taste all over (shops, restaurant, employees). Of course nothing beats visiting the country, but as I said, if you're there just on a layover, you can pretty much leave taking some Brazilian flavour with you'.

'What about the easiest to use?

The newly built terminal at Bogotá's El Dorado is a state of the art building like no other I've seen in South America. You would never say you are in a country that is still struggling to find peace after decades of a domestic war with guerrilla groups and drug lords. It reminds me rather of a European hub, being a modern glass and steel construction with huge, wide areas to wander, nice passenger waiting zones, world class services, shops and duty free, and very well designed airline lounges.

'The growth of Avianca is behind this, especially after the merger with TACA. They were having a huge competition against TAM and LAN and were benefiting from the strategic geographical position of Colombia, closer to the Northern Hemisphere than Sao Paulo and Santiago. Bogotá is a very easy and user friendly airport for connections, either domestic or international; a seamless experience. When you book a flight from the US to South America, chances are that the cheapest fares that will pop up will be the ones via Colombia. Also there are excellent views of the airside, of the main runway, and all the gates. Great for taking pictures during a layover, no matter how long or short it is'.

Which does raise an interesting point; 'How difficult is it to take photographs at South and Central American airports generally?' I asked. 'What recommendations would you make to European enthusiasts wanting to make a trip? Personally whenever I go to an airport I tend to try and make it an official visit, which they usually are these days since its often for a magazine article, or even a book (like this one)'.

'You play well on the safe side if you do it that way, Kevan', he grinned. 'In my case, I do it as a hobby, so I try to sneak around and blend as a tourist as much as I can. When I was travelling for work as a journalist, it was too obvious as I had my professional gear with me and any official or airport's workers would ask me if I had permission, thinking it was for commercial purposes, so I refrained from doing it to avoid getting in trouble.

'So the general rule is not to appear too obvious. Taking pictures inside the terminal building (check-in and baggage claim areas or security zones) is a no-no, as you will most likely be approached and asked not to, or even interrogated. Once past security and in the boarding areas, it's much more reasonable and understandable if you take photographs — again, remember to blend as a tourist who is on holiday and enjoying whatever catches your eye's attention.

'If you plan on spotting at airplanes coming and going around the airport, better don't hang around the same spot for a long time, and never too close to the perimeter fence. Being a foreigner helps and sometimes the language barrier may be even better than speaking the local language because this might encourage the security people to engage in a longer interrogatory to you. While generally they know that foreigners like to take a lot of photographs and if they see they cannot communicate fluidly, they might let you go as soon as they're comfortable with what you were doing, which can happen pretty quickly'.

'So what are your favourite Latin American airports and why?'

'For me it's Sao Paulo, of course. It is the most important one in terms of connectivity in the continent. And no doubt it is the most 'global' one of the entire Latin American region. What I mean by this is you can get flights from there to the most relevant airports in Europe and the US, but also you can easily spot aircraft of Emirates, Qatar, El Al, South African, Turkish and even Korean Air, meaning you have flights to Dubai, Doha, Tel Aviv, Johannesburg, Istanbul and Seoul. Quite impressive considering this place is so far away from almost everywhere else in the world.

Of course, the local TAM airlines (now LATAM) also has lots of transcontinental connections and we cannot forget Sao Paulo is also linked to almost all domestic Brazilian airports, all the South American major airports and many more in Central America and the Caribbean. So you have there a wide variety of carriers that truly makes it a world-class airport. In Central America, Panama City's Tocumen is one of my most favoured. Over the years, it has transformed into a very efficient hub for Copa Airlines, whose strategy you can see working. It's not that big, so connecting is easy and fast, and most likely you won't have to walk much. Problem is it can get pretty crowded at rush hours, and since it's not large, you can feel a little cramped finding your way to the gate. The Duty Free area is all scattered and you have the feeling at times that you are at a street mall in Miami. Flights to the Caribbean - they all depart from Tocumen, as do most of the South American and Central American capitals.

'Interestingly enough, last time I was there I was a taking a TAP flight to Lisbon. You can also get Air France to Paris CDG, KLM to Amsterdam or Iberia to Madrid, not to mention the star of the show, the intended Emirates flight to Dubai, which will be the longest non-stop route in the world. Also, San Jose, Costa Rica and San Salvador have turned into very friendly connection hubs, especially the latter, after Avianca and TACA merged and reinforced San Salvador as an important regional hub. It used to be the hub for TACA - it still is, but with the Avianca merger, planes are now smaller and you don't see that much activity as before.

'Funny thing is if you are in the region, let's say in Nicaragua and need to go to neighbouring Guatemala you will most likely fly via San Salvador. The activity is a frenzy when all the flights come and leave and the connections are at their peak. It is a small terminal and very easy to move around. And since aircraft that fly in and out are not that big, then you don't get to see huge crowds.

'On the sad side, one airport I think might be worth mentioning is Caracas. They used to call themselves the Gateway of the Americas. This was my home airport for 10 years in the 70's, when I was growing up. Those were the times when even Air France had a regular Concorde flight scheduled from Paris. Venezuela was booming and everything looked so promising. But the country's economy has collapsed in the past recent years and the situation has prompted several international carriers to drop their service to Caracas, since the government won't allow them to get their benefits due to the strict currency exchange regulations. They have suspended service and some others have dramatically cut the capacity (American, United, Caribbean Airlines). The result is an almost empty terminal, with very little traffic compared to what there should be and, of course, to what they were dreaming of in the 70's and 80's.

'No question really, it is sad, as was the bankruptcy of VIASA, the former Venezuelan national airline', I agreed. 'How about anywhere else - which airports elsewhere around the world rank highly for you?'

'I fell in love with Osaka Kansai during my first trip there, in 1998, three years after its opening. I was fascinated by the fact that it was built on an artificial island of land reclamation, with all the engineering work that that involved. I was not disappointed at all, and I have seen very few alike since. I also enjoy very much other Asian airports like Singapore, Hong Kong and Peking. They have a distinctive atmosphere and a sense of efficiency and cleanliness all over. Munich and Amsterdam are my two favourite in Europe, and I have some special attraction for Dubai, whose impressive growth awes me. I also love London Heathrow for the great variety of carriers and all the biggies that visit often from any corner of the planet. It really makes me feel like a world citizen just by seeing all these airlines from countries you only dream about visiting someday'.

'Do you get to fly to Europe much currently?'

'Not currently, but I have until about a year ago. Out of all the 344 airports I've been to, 118 are in Europe, which is roughly less than a third of them. I am very happy to have visited Keflavik, which serves the northernmost capital in

Conversation

the world, Reykjavík, and also a few of them you don't usually log as a tourist, thanks to my profession as a journalist, like Sarajevo [Bosnia and Herzegovina], Ercan, Northern Cyprus, Pristina, in Kosovo, or Rostov-on-Don, in southern Russia, apart from a few other landing strips and fields not even marked as regular airports.

'When all these low-cost carriers began flourishing in Europe, I found that as an opportunity to fly in and out of many airports that were not even in my plans before. So I loved going to places such as Saarbrucken (Germany), Eindhoven and Rotterdam in the Netherlands, East Midlands, Bristol and Prestwick in the UK, Sandefjord in Norway and Billund, Denmark just to name a few, and I proudly show them now in my airports map'.

'How about Miami?' I queried. Its an obvious one since its Pablo's home and it has changed a lot since I was last there. 'It was always a hot-spot for people wanting to get photographs of South and Central American airlines, and the north side was famous for old aircraft. Not so much these days, since the third parallel runway was built'.

'It still is the place where you can be sure get all the Central American and South American carriers, only there *is* no more 'all the Central American and South American carriers'. What I mean by this...' he grinned mischievously, '...is we only have two airlines from Central America; Avianca-TACA aircraft are slowly being repainted with Avianca colours and the other is Copa, meaning no more Honduran, Nicaraguan, Guatemalan or Costa Rican carriers around. From South America, LAN Chile and TAM Brazil merged and, together with Avianca, dominate the scene. You can still see BOA (Boliviana de Aviación) and Aerolíneas Argentinas. No more Peruvian (absorbed by LAN, now Latam) or Paraguayan (absorbed by TAM, also now Latam), while Ecuadorian carrier TAME flies to neighbouring FLL.

'Also, there are a few Venezuelan carriers (SBA, Avior and Laser) and beautiful Surinam Airways. From the Caribbean there is PAWA Dominicana, Insel, Cayman Airways and Bahamasair. No more Air Jamaica or BWIA from past times, Kevan, as they both fly now under the Caribbean Airlines name and, sadly, they are getting rid of the beautiful hummingbird that decorated their planes' tails until very recently.

'American Airlines has its main operations for Latin America based in Miami, and is a big hub for the airline too, connecting traffic from the rest of the country to South and Central America. Interestingly enough, Miami has a decent amount of European carriers, as well as Qatar and Turkish Airlines. Three A-380's visit here regularly (Lufthansa, British Airways and Air France) and the French airline has an A-320 based in Miami, operating a route to Papeete and Fort de France, arguably making Miami the only airport in the country where you can spot an Air France A320.

'Yes, you are right in that there are not many old aircraft on the north side, which is mainly where all the cargo companies are now. But you can still see a few Convair 580 and Boeing 727s, cargo of course. No more DC-8s or Boeing 707s or others, but still a fair amount of DC-10s/MD-11s, Airbus 300s and Boeing 747s or 767-200s. Cargo operations are fairly important to MIA, which gives the airport an additional interest and colours as well as heavy traffic'.

I pondered the wave of mergers, take-overs, bankruptcies and disappearance of so many of South America's traditional airlines – its not so very different in the US or Europe, so much has changed in commercial aviation over the past decade or more. Brazil's VARIG went, being replaced by TAM and that airline's growth, then merging with LAN of Chile making the group probably the most powerful in South America and then there is Colombia's Avianca and its rise. Its much the same with Air France/KLM or British Airways and Iberia. Change of subject...

'There's a great story brewing over runway expansion in London. How much attention is that getting in your part of the world? Not to mention the UK referendum result and leaving the EU. That last point does seem to have caused something of a stir worldwide'.

'We're always looking at Europeans to see how they behave and what they decide, especially when it comes to politics. The Brexit referendum shocked everyone here, and was widely compared to the Peace referendum in Colombia that happened later, where all the odds were in favour of the popular support for the agreement between the government and the FARC guerrilla movement, yet it resulted in the voters rejecting it. So all the comparisons were in place... the UK and Colombia, what went wrong (or right) and why no one predicted it?

'So in the world of Aviation here, the expansion of LHR is seen as a pioneer in the effort of overcoming the hurdles. LHR is a great airport, admired by many, and the expansion will only make it shine even brighter so it can hopefully keep being 'our' favourite international world airport. Particularly, I've always been fascinated by Heathrow as the most diverse international airport. There's never a dull moment spotting there and it happens to be the airport where I took the first one of my two Concorde supersonic flights. I've flown in and out of LHR a total of forty-six times, which puts it number nine in my list of airports, ahead of important ones like Chicago O'Hare, Washington Dulles, Amsterdam or even Caracas, which was my home airport as a kid'.

'So what's next? Where do you think you'll be over the next few years? Are you likely to start covering aviation as a journalist more?'

'I want to take advantage of my more extensive knowledge and means to pursue my Aviation hobby and live it to the fullest. I now have a lot of fun just taking plane spotting/photography trips, like to Iran, Hong Kong, Dubai and Helicopter Spotting in Los Angeles just during my last year, and have some other interesting ones cooking for the next few months.

'Sometimes I think I would love to make a living out of my hobby. I started thinking about it back in 1996 or so, when, thanks to the Internet, I learned about how many people like me were out there indeed, and realized I was not the only one crazy about Commercial Aviation. I always think about going to all these places and airports I've been to, and many more, as well as talking to the officials with the airlines I've flown to be able to really have access to a lot of interesting information and transmit it to the public. At times I think it could be a nice way to retire, and at times I think I'd rather keep it as a hobby.

'I always think about living a retired life just for the airplanes, you know, like watching them, photographing them, flying them anywhere in the world. We all like dreaming, don't we?'

.

Guatemala City *(Pablo Herrera)*

Award-winning Quito (Pablo Herrera)

Panama City (Pablo Herrera)

11
UK Wings III

A commercial aircraft is a vehicle capable of supporting itself aerodynamically and economically at the same time

William B. Stout, designer of the Ford Tri-Motor

FJ
Birmingham Airport (BHX), formerly known as Birmingham International - and not to be confused with Birmingham, Alabama - is located in Solihull, a few miles from the city of Birmingham itself and serves an array of destinations, including those in North America, the Caribbean and the Indian Subcontinent, as well as Europe and UK domestic destinations. Airlines based at BHX include Flybe, Monarch, Ryanair, Thomas Cook and Thomson and it is also served by airlines such as Qatar Airways, Icelandair, Emirates and Pakistan International Airlines, among others.

My first visit to Birmingham came toward the end of April 2016, when I met up with some friends for a day trip for photography at Dublin, flying with Ryanair. It was busy when we flew but we got through security quickly and airside. It is a pleasant airport with a terminal that affords good views and we spent a pleasant half hour taking photos through the terminal window, including a Thomson 787, a Qatar Airways 787 and a Monarch A321. It was a very cold morning so we also could watch the deicing activities that were going on. A security guard and his gorgeous Springer Spaniel, trained for sniffing out drugs and other contraband, passed by but wished us good morning, agreed it was a good place to watch and photograph the action and let us pet the dog.

Boarding our Ryanair flight was fairly quick and painless, our passports were checked and we went down a ramp before walking across the tarmac and up the stairs of a brand-new Boeing 737 that was to take us on the short hop over the Irish Sea. This was my first trip to Ireland and I would like to return for a longer visit sometime but I have other travel priorities to see to first.

On our return from Dublin, we were off the plane and out of the airport in very little time and it is a quick bus ride to the nearby long-stay car park. I was dropped off by my friends back at my hotel, a Travelodge in Halesowen that was more like a university halls of residence as I remembered from my student days, but it was comfortable enough and adequate for a night or two.

The next day, Sunday, I returned to BHX for more photos before driving back to south London for work but the day began in disastrous fashion when, on exiting the multi storey car park at a local supermarket where I had stopped to get something to eat, I managed to hit a steel support girder that was in my blind spot and do some substantial damage to the right side wing panel and bumper of my car. After it was pushed back together I continued - in a very bad mood - to the airport (the repairs required a whole new front end and my insurance premium doubled overnight).

That day's spotting place was yet another multi-storey, next to the terminal, complete with pillars in awkward places and this luckily didn't involve any more arguments with support structures or lamp posts - although I did get to witness another driver doing the *exact same thing* I had done an hour previously when he side-swiped a badly-placed concrete lamp post when he tried to leave!

During my short time at BHX, I managed to get a few photos of arriving aircraft and the multi storey car park was a good vantage point and is great with good weather. It is easy to get to, located in Terminal Road just off the A45 Coventry Road and close to the M42.

KJ

Heathrow's Terminal 5 at night is eerie. The airport never closes but it does have a 'last flight' and a 'first flight', the final movements being before midnight and the first arrival at T5, at least on this occasion, due at 4.50am, from Hong Kong. Given how it throngs with activity during the day such a vast space so empty is, as one of the police officers on patrol put it, 'weird'. There are airports elsewhere in the world that, because of their location within the air transport system, see a lot of night time use. Noise restrictions in Europe mean that most flights depart or arrive during the time when people tend to be awake and doing things but those restrictions are paid for further east along the airways. The same noise issues arise on the other side of the world in Australia, which means that airports at each end of round the world flights are buzzing during the day - and empty at night. There are a few waiting passengers sleeping in the floor and a small number uncomfortably dozing on the chairs, of which there aren't many. But it does at least give me a chance to chat to people who aren't normally there during the day.

Having seen the police arrive to do their rounds I showed them my press card and said why I was there. No problems with some ethereal photographs of an almost empty T5 and we parted saying we'd look out for each other later. When later came they were with another three officers and somebody from the airport so I asked if I could have a chat. Apparently, despite their being in a group, they were dealing with a 'minor incident' so weren't able to talk then. They would be happy to later if they came across me again however. Whatever the incident was, it passed unnoticed by everybody else. The airport continued its slumbers undisturbed.

I did have a brief conversation with one of the airport's Assistant Facility Managers, a chap named Prabs, and he made the point that T5 is open 24 hours a day, every day of the week. Interestingly, although less of an issue in the summer, the homeless are not thrown out at night. In winter when temperatures are hovering around freezing, provided somebody with no place to go behaves themselves there is not an issue. Those that do show up for the most part just sleep. There isn't a problem with the homeless at Heathrow generally and although it is not public property, T5 is a public building and thus open to the public – the key is to behave with a little thought and consideration towards others, most of whom, despite their small numbers, are there because they want to use the building for its intended purpose. The public TVs are on, showing BBC's news 24 channel and there are public internet facilities; you get 20 minutes free internet access.

I had a quick word with a chap who is driving a cleaning machine up and down since the machine doesn't appear to actually do anything. It seems the device does its stuff without water since it would take too long to dry properly so all night he drives this thing along the terminal, cleaning and polishing the floor as he goes. Otherwise, the only people around are hard-hat wearing workmen doing something at the southern end of the building and a small number of mostly sleeping passengers waiting for early flights. One of those awake was Taylor, a college student from Iowa in the USA, who is using mileage credits for a European trip; it doesn't get you the best flight times so he had arrived earlier that day on an American Airlines flight from Chicago O'Hare and had a twelve hour wait for his onward BA flight to Frankfurt. Still, he had his ipad and everything else so there he was. Waiting…waiting…waiting. Just like me and others. How many people are there doing the same in airports the world over?

Taylor is studying to be a Doctor and hasn't yet decided what to specialise in but says he is not a fan of air travel especially, preferring to get in and out of airports as quickly as possible. Most passengers are the same – the flight is just the best way of going from one place to another and the terminal a place to pass through.

One of the good things about late spring and summer are short nights. As the sky lightens, the airport comes alive. In T5 the massive computer-driven advertising displays either side of the security channels spark into life (they begin with the words 'Microsoft is starting up' before anything else appears…) Aircraft parked on the apron overnight have doors opened and start to look as though they will be going somewhere soon. Ground crews appear around them and the terminal begins to fill, mostly at first, by people wearing uniforms - in the case of T5 British Airways uniforms. Early passengers arrive, looking anxious, looking hurried, looking businesslike or just looking. The huge sprawl of T5 for some is a big space and they need to know where to go. The seasoned traveller already knows. Prabs goes off duty, the cleaner goes home, his machine stored somewhere in the bowels of T5 and Taylor gets to go to Frankfurt. I'm going to Leeds.

(image courtesy of Birmingham Airport)

BHX Birmingham Elmdon

England's 'second city' is admirably served at BHX with an increasingly diverse range of airlines and with high-speed train links, could relieve pressure on the London airports.

Above and main image - dawn to dusk; as well as long haul services by carriers such as Qatar Airways, short haul scheduled, holiday and UK domestic flights are also frequent. *(Fay Johnson)*

Above - BHX has a well-equipped and comfortable terminal *(Birmingham Airport)*

Overnighting

There are times when one has to be at an airport at night...

Heathrow's T5 is a vast and empty space except for the floor cleaners, the early am store deliveries and a lonely luggage trolley. At least until dawn and breakfast at Caffe Nero *(all images Kevan James)*

Far too early in the morning...
Heathrow Terminal 5 *(Kevan James)*

T5's vast spaces don't appear anywhere near as big when filled with people and by the time of boarding flight BA1340, even this humongous and still relatively new people-processing plant is a hive of busyness. Flight crews scurry to gates and passengers wait. Despite its size, and opening only in 2008, T5 is now not big enough for all of British Airways' flights so the airline has re-established a sizeable long-hail operation at its old home in Terminal 3. Something of a deja-vu moment perhaps since BA left T3 in 1986 when T4 opened. That too ultimately proved too small for Heathrow's home airline.

T3 does not however have, and has never had, any domestic facilities so what is now left of once fairly comprehensive UK links to Heathrow is limited to Manchester, Belfast, Glasgow, Edinburgh, Newcastle, Leeds Bradford (LBA) and, as of 2016, reinstated services to Inverness, all served by British Airways from T5. Gone are services to the Channel Islands of Jersey and Guernsey, the Isle of Man, Aberdeen, East Midlands, Liverpool and others. Of those currently served, Manchester is the nearest at 151 miles and it remains the third busiest in the UK after the London airports of Heathrow and Gatwick. One can only wonder how long it will be before it too will go, since it is around two and a half hours by train and still, at the time of writing with just two runways, pressure on space at Heathrow continues to grow. The slots currently occupied by flights to Manchester might well be better used – from an airline's point of view – for more lucrative longer services. Manchester, like Leeds Bradford and almost all other UK airports also have direct links to places like Amsterdam, Paris and Frankfurt. Passengers wanting to go elsewhere in the world do not have to travel via Heathrow and given the short distance between Heathrow and Manchester unless there is more runway capacity in London and at Heathrow in particular, UK services will come under yet more scrutiny. Those other UK airports still served from Heathrow do at least have some distance in their favour making it more viable, at least from the time taken to fly point of view, more equable and more competitive with regard connecting for longer flights to other parts of the globe.

But not Manchester. Or Leeds

Leeds Bradford Airport is 173 miles from Heathrow and just 35 minutes flying time. An hour is given for the duration, which is actually from terminal gate to terminal gate. Today it's a long way from T5 to the other end of the airport for departure on runway 27 left. Once in the air, the cabin crew serve bacon butties and tea; they haven't got long and short flights like this one are the flights that make crews, both cabin and cockpit, work hardest. There is no time to pause – get the refreshments served, remains collected and strap in for landing. This morning's flight is about half full so it does give a very efficient and friendly set of flight attendants a little more time.

Leeds Bradford bills itself as 'Yorkshire's Gateway Airport', and although there are others in the county, it is the busiest and largest; serving 3.4m passengers a year with 70 direct destinations across 23 countries. Manchester is geographically not far away from LBA but separating the two are the Pennines, those undulating hills and valleys that make the road journey between them sometimes a little time-consuming. If one lives in Yorkshire, particularly the eastern side of the county, LBA is a better bet and the airport continually strives to attract as many Yorkshire people as possible though its doors through the widening choices available for passengers jetting off from the region.

Like many regional airports, LBA still has its original terminal. Extended at either end with modern additions, the central part has a cosy and undeniably lovely historic feel to it and all gates are just a five minute walk from security. There is greater pressure on aircraft parking space, with LBA's home carrier Jet 2 being responsible for a substantial part of the airport's growth in recent years. The airline flies to more than 45 leisure destinations and the northern extension to the terminal is exclusively Jet 2, its bright red colours vividly illustrating the airline's status as the home-town airline. British Airways are doing well with their three-times-daily link to Heathrow, the first and last flights giving those doing business almost a full day in the capital (and often the other way around). Having the ability to connect onto long haul flights at Heathrow T5 is also a positive to Leeds Bradford's British Airways schedule. Amsterdam's Schipol airport, with KLM being a major player at LBA, is also another option for passengers looking for long-haul options, as they are at most UK airports. For flights across the Atlantic, Aer Lingus also connect the Yorkshire airport to Dublin with onward connections to five destinations in the USA along with Toronto in Canada and Spain's Vueling also offer 160 onward connections from their Barcelona hub.

LBA's Aviation Development Director, Tony Hallwood, is understandably enthusiastic about the airport and is supportive of a new runway at Heathrow.

'The London connection is one of our most important, the route is doing well and LBA has the largest catchment area outside of London,' he said. 'More than three million people live within a thirty-minute drive of LBA.'

There is a new Masterplan being finalised for expansion at LBA, which does not include lengthening the existing runway but has ambitions to extend the apron. The vision for LBA is to carry 7.1m passengers by 2030 and to be able to offer a real mix of leisure and business destinations. That will mean some terminal development, which will see apron expansion, an economic hub nearby, a hotel onsite and new surface access via road and rail.

'With new aircraft like the Boeing 787, the runway length isn't the crucial factor it once was', Tony continued. 'We'd be keen to add long haul services here and we have the capacity to handle additional services with smaller long range types - like the 787, which can fit within our existing facilities.'

I'm curious about there being just two air bridges in use at LBA. 'We don't anticipate needing more so have no current plans to add any", replied Tony. "The pair we have are mostly used by British Airways and KLM but we do have a covered walkway to the other terminal gates, mostly used by Jet 2 and our other airlines'.

On a purely personal note, I like the idea, on a warm sunny day, of using old-style steps to get on and off an aircraft, letting the sounds and aromas of commercial aviation waft over me and even more so if I can get some interesting photographs out of it *(I know the feeling - TMcD)*. But on a cold and wet winter's day it might not be so appealing.

Unusually, the pair of bridges at LBA do not carry the logo of a well-known worldwide banking corporation (found almost everywhere, including Heathrow and Gatwick) but on the outer side, facing the incoming aircraft, boldly proclaim 'Welcome to Leeds Bradford Airport' and on the other, thus facing the terminal and waiting passengers, one carries the name and logo of British Airways, the other KLM - an indication perhaps, of the two airlines standing in the commercial aviation world and at LBA.

Leeds Bradford is a welcoming and friendly regional UK airport that, for some time in the past at least, was a little underserved in some respects, although it has always had a good range of services. Today, it has a bright future and with a dedicated and enthusiastic team in place running it and knowing how to make it fit into an increasingly global marketplace, it's a part of the UK worth going to - the historic City of York, the Yorkshire Dales, not to mention the two cities after which the airport is named.

Before flying back to Heathrow's T5, I spent some time in the airport's Yorkshire Premier Lounge, which has been recently upgraded and expanded. For departing passengers this is a real bonus and offers a great relaxing or working space ahead of the journey.

The internet has provided people with the means to contact airports directly and ask for information, even if not aviation enthusiasts, flight times being an obvious reason and like almost all airports today, Leeds Bradford has its own website (www.leedsbradfordairport.co.uk) and although one can find out a lot from them, including flight schedules, nothing beats actually going somewhere and seeing things for yourself. One of the benefits of writing about aviation for a living is meeting people who run airports. My time at LBA was brief but informative and as we parted, Tony said, 'Thank you for visiting us.'

That's how Yorkshire people are; warm and friendly and it included some of those with whom I had brief conversations working in the terminal and a couple waiting for their own flight – the traditional Yorkshire welcome.

∎

Leeds Bradford
Yorkshire

British Airways, with its daily services to Heathrow, and KLM, linking their hub at Amsterdam, are two of the major users of Leeds Bradford, along with Jet2.com for whom the airport is home. Unusually the airbridges carry the airline names but only on the inside. The outside carries the airport's own **message** *(all images Kevan James)*

Top left; As one of the UK's smaller regional airports, Leeds Bradford's terminal doesn't have the size or scale found elsewhere so wherever one goes one can feel the welcome.
Top right; Check in facilities are on the left side of the main terminal.
Centre; comfort and relaxation in the Premier Lounge.
Bottom right: Naturally the Yorkshire Welcome extends to younger travellers.
Main image; to the left of the original terminal, a more modern extension is where check in facilties for all airlines is found.
(all images Kevan James)

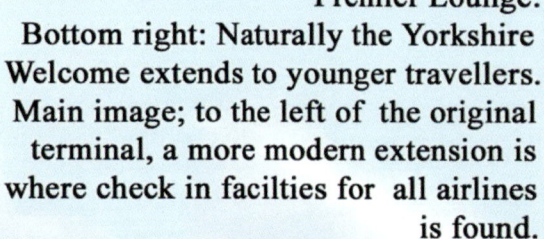

Above and left - locally based Jet2.com has built a Europe-wide network from Leeds Bradford and is the airport's primary carrier. The right hand side of the terminal contains the airline's own check in hall.

Below - terminal advertisment; travellers to the U.S.A. can take advantage of Aer Lingus and the short hop to Dublin to connect to six destinations across the Atlantic

(images Kevan James)

Aer Lingus

The new way to the USA

12
Who Shouts the Loudest?

If you don't read the newspaper you are uninformed. If you do read the newspaper you are misinformed.

Mark Twain

KJ

On Tuesday 25 October, 2016, the Government finally ended 70 years of dithering and announced a decision on airport expansion, giving Heathrow to go-ahead to build a third runway.

Predictably there was instant reaction from all and sundry, with the great and the good (those with the clout to get their names and faces on TV and in print media) pronouncing the decision undeliverable, bad, awful, noisy and so on and so forth. Business leaders commended the decision and, perhaps significantly, especially those in Scotland. Social media was awash with comments, some in favour, some not and many remarks, despite their passion and enthusiasm for commercial aviation (and perhaps even reading this book) not well informed either.

The biggest mass of commentary on social media, particularly Facebook (although there were others), came from enthusiasts wanting...no, demanding even, that Heathrow include spotting facilities as part of the development. Numerous responses made the point that Heathrow is about making a profit and is not interested in spotters. So let's start there...

Heathrow Airport Limited (HAL) is indeed a privately owned company, as are the airlines that use it. Like those airlines, it has to make money or fail – whether one cares to concede the point or not, that is the nature of business. Think of the great names of the airline world that failed to adapt to a changing industry and went bust; Pan American and Swissair to name just two. Even state-owned airlines, like Sabena of Belgium and Hungary's Malev, went to the wall because they had become failing businesses. Ryanair boss Michael O'Leary may well be a love-him-or-hate-him figure to some, but he is a smart man and knows how to make his business model work, which is why Ryanair is now one of Europe's biggest airlines. And there are smart people running HAL.

HAL is not, as many think, uninterested in spotters and enthusiasts. For many watchers of airliners that may be a difficult concept to grasp but consider this; HAL have been tasked with rebuilding Heathrow Airport and its new terminals demonstrate their capability for doing just that; the airport is today an award-winning, high-value piece of essential transport infrastructure, with those awards including work on the environment and noise pollution (despite those who conveniently ignore that aspect of HAL's work). The company has had to do so while running an airport that still ranks as one of the world's greatest, serving one of the world's greatest cities. They have had to do it whilst under constant, unrelenting pressure from those who would seemingly rather have no airport at all, decades of Government indecision and interference, and, most significantly of all, pressure from those who would happily kill as many innocent airport users as they can. Amongst those users by the way, is you.

HAL's priority has been to rebuild an airport that is safe to use, as secure as it can be, as efficient as it is possible to be, as comfortable for passengers as it can made to be and one that stands on its own two feet financially. Everything else is secondary-including enthusiasts. Yes, it is done elsewhere, but elsewhere is not London and along with New York, London remains a prime target for terrorists. Heathrow has been the subject of numerous attacks in the past, none of which, up to the time of writing, have succeeded. For that, every reader of this book, whether a watcher of planes, a passenger or both, must offer some thanks to HAL and the Metropolitan Police for our safety, on the ground and in the air.

So can something be done to make Heathrow as good to visit for the enthusiast as are Amsterdam, Frankfurt or Zurich? Of course it can. And be in no doubt, at some point, however long away it may be, times will change and there will come a day when there will be somewhere safe, secure, supervised and official, for spotters to go and watch, take photographs and just enjoy the atmosphere of Heathrow, and have a good view. With the size of an expanded airport, perhaps even more than one - but that time has not yet come. Before it does, HAL will have to secure its perimeters not only from terrorists but from protesters against its very existence as well as against a new runway – every time somebody tries or successfully breaks into Heathrow, London City or anywhere else, no matter how passionate they may be, and perhaps even well-meaning too, their actions adversely affect the thousands more whose interest is entirely lawful and legitimate.

Is there any significance in the fact that the two London airports that have had their operational areas breached most recently are Heathrow and City? With both sharing the same enthusiasts Identity card scheme? Probably not – but the existence of the ID card scheme is a good one and anybody who hasn't got one should apply for one immediately. It won't get you a viewing area and it won't stop you being moved away from sensitive areas, but it does at least show you are who you say you are – and the more people who do sign up to the idea, the more likely it is that greater efforts can ultimately be justified to gain, or regain, those lost areas that real enthusiasts would like.

So what happens next with the third runway? Actually, not very much; there is a year long statutory consultation period, but even so, HAL will be putting in place the plans to get things moving at the earliest opportunity. Some twelve months from October 2016 MPs will be given a free vote on the final outcome so if you really are an aviation lover and a user (however infrequent), make your views known to your local MP, even if its one who says he or she is opposed to runway expansion at Heathrow. Its also worth pointing out that had the decision been given to Gatwick, the protestations would be just as vocal. Stansted has already been there, as has Manchester when its second runway was built. Slipping in under the radar as it were is the almost unremarked upon extension to London City Airport's terminal; the area south of the runway will soon be closed off as the building grows to the east and what is now the watery basin that once was filled with cargo-carrying ships from around the world will fill instead with a bigger terminal, but it is needed and it will be built.

So will a new runway at Heathrow. Or at Gatwick or even at both. Because they have to be – at some point.

It has been said by some that if Heathrow builds a new runway, 'they will then want another one...' To properly serve both London and the country as a whole, one fact cannot be denied; Heathrow needs two new runways rather than one and Gatwick also needs a second. There is a strong case for a second at Stansted as well. Undoubtedly former London Mayor Boris Johnson (along with many others) will go apoplectic should he read those words but stop for a moment...Johnson himself was a strong advocate of a completely new airport, known as 'Boris Island' with...four runways.

The UK and its capital city needs four new runways and it needs them now, not in ten years, or twenty years or however long it takes the British to get anything done. Once built, a four-runway Heathrow, with two at both Gatwick and Stansted, a total of six, will not see a requirement for any more thereafter simply because there will be no more room in the air to accommodate more aircraft. The air corridors will be full and there is no room to make those aerial roads bigger, despite the apparent emptiness of the sky.

And the reason for having those runways – and expanded terminals - is to get aircraft out of that sky and on the ground, or away from their departure airport and on their way to wherever they are going.

The simple fact is that the fewer runways there are, the more time aircraft will spend going round in circles over London waiting to land or lining up on the taxiway, all with engines running, fuel being used and emitting emissions (even though both are much, much lower than they once were) waiting to depart.

Whoever shouts the loudest…

LHR
Heathrow

The Queen's Terminal T2

All life passes by in an airport terminal yet for some - main image - it is always playtime.
Left - waiting...arriving.
Centre left - elevating
Below - waiting...departing

(all images Kevan James)

heathrow
London
T3

The 1969 747 Pier still stands but like the terminal itself, the airline names have changed over the years. New carriers ply routes from elsewhere around the globe and some of Europe's most well-established airlines now use Terminal 3. Although essentially the same building, today's T3 looks very different from the original 1950s design.
(all images Tyler McDowell except top right, Kevan James)

Terminal 4 celebrated it's 30th anniversary in 2017, the same year that the airport reached 70 years.
(main image and lower left - Kevan James, top left and right images - Tyler McDowell)

T5 LHR

Terminal 5 had some issues when it opened but has since become an efficient and comfortable place in which to start or end one's flight.
(all images Kevan James except below right, Tyler McDowell)

Welcome to Terminal 5

Flight

the terminal
(Kevan James)

13
Flight

It is only with the heart that one can see clearly. What is essential is invisible to the eye.

Antoine de Saint Exupéry

KJ

There was a time, not too long ago, when flying was, for many people, a relatively relaxing, if occasionally bumpy, way to travel. One would turn up, check in, wait for a short while, then amble on board and fly. There have always been those who love flight and those who don't, just as there are those who love driving or travelling by train. There are those who not only dislike flying but are physically unable to board a plane because of their fear of flying. A number of airlines offer those most afraid of flight a 'get familiar' day out when they can experience the whole kit and caboodle; talks by airline personnel and others, videos explaining who does what and how an aircraft stays in the air - and at the end of it, if they feel they can, a short flight in a real airliner. For most, it is a successful day and they fly. The fear is however, understandable.

Flying is humanity's most alien environment since space travel is not yet commonplace and we have the ability, should we choose to learn, to swim and float when in water. But we can't fly. At least, not without the help of what is undeniably a miracle of modern and yet also historic technology. It has been said many times but always worth repeating, that flying is outstandingly the safest way of travelling. Despite the lurid headlines of sensationalist news print media, despite the scare stories and doom-mongering of some, most people stand more chance of death or injury at home and definitely in a road vehicle than in an airliner.

Because flying is still so beyond our capabilities without the assistance of invention, the nature of flight gives rise to the strongest emotions and perhaps even more so given that things are not what they used to be. The procedures for riding an airliner have changed beyond recognition when compared to how they once were. One's reasons for merely being at an airport are now questioned whereas once they were not. Yesterday's years are gone, and as aviation enthusiasts once knew them, probably for good.

There has always been a deadline for checking in, another for reaching the departure gate - miss them and you miss your flight. Just as it is for the train or bus; arrive late for either, they leave, you stay. It takes longer today than it did to board a flight, whether it is from London to Leeds, Boston to Baku, Toronto to Tallin. A man will arrive breathless at the airport, to see his flight still there, its departure time yet to come, but he is denied boarding because he is too late for check in. His emotions may get the better of him and airline staff bear the brunt of his distress. The Roman philosopher Seneca wrote, for the benefit of Emperor Nero, that the root cause of anger is hope. We are angry because we are overly optimistic, unprepared for the frustrations that arise when things do not go as we feel they should - and there are circumstances that apply today that did not apply yesterday. So it takes longer than it did to check in, go through security, be checked yet again and all airports and airlines now look differently at their customers and what they carry with them; the innocent carton of juice, the child's doll and the weary yet smiling wrinkles of Grandma and Granddad.

Flight

To one degree or another people accept the inconvenience of the security check line, the removal of shoes and belts, the questions from those doing the checking and the anxiety of watching one's personal belongings, carried because they mean something, disappear into the uninviting darkness of a machine that scans intimately each and every item.

The efficiency of those doing the security checks has been tested, perhaps once in a decade for real, more often by somebody checking the checkers. Journalists - and book authors - have long been enamoured of the idea of access, that a free press means an unfettered and unrestricted way past the barriers erected against mere mortals but we are bound by the same rules as everybody else. Granted our reasons for doing something may differ from others in that we subsequently write about what see and what we experience; I have carried out my own test of airport security by placing two empty plastic bottles in a regulation sized carry-on bag at two different airports – on both occasions, they were seen and commented on. On a third occasion the two bottles were taken out of my bag and placed in the tray for the machine to examine. Bottles and I flew - my reasoning for having them accepted. Even so, our fantasy that the revealing of a national photo-identification press card means the guard puts away his armament and waves us through is not the route to secrets shared.

Unceasing vigilance against the terrorist keeps us safe and other than looking from the outside in as we pass through, the means by which we are kept safe remain as they must and as they should – a necessary enigma of air travel, even to book authors and journalists.

Once past security (the feeling that we have beaten the system sometimes makes one want to dance the jig of the victorious – *I did it! I'm going on my plane today!*), an even bigger barrier to our flight presents itself with the shopping mall and for perhaps too many, the lure of the airport bar. With time to spare for those who, at least thus far, have played by the rules and arrived early, the temptation is great and the result is sometimes a frantic last-minute search for a missing passenger or two and the bar is the first place to look.

There are times when the missing remain so and the flight is delayed while the bags of the absent are removed from the flight; no aircraft takes off without the bag's owner on board.

The airport mall is the place for picking up the last-minute item, and very often the obvious thing that one needs but forgot. More alluring than the High Street (even if the prices may not be) the airport terminal shops and stores can part the unwary from their money with remarkable ease; it depends on the individual, how much spare cash they may have and how strong-willed they are but airport stores are very welcoming places. The number of shops now found within an airport terminal has been criticised by some but they are one of the means by which an airport makes money and stays operational. Yet how many critics have visited their local mall for no reason other than its existence? The mall is there so go to it and simply browse. There is no compulsion to buy just as there is no mandatory requirement to spend one's money at the airport - even though the temptation may be stronger given that many people are not in their natural place when in one. They may well feel at home when peering through the local mall's windows but not when travelling. Which may be the point, the airport shop's reason for being; not merely to remove money from one's purse or wallet but also to make one feel more normal, more as though one feels under any usual circumstance. The only difference is the absence from the local mall of the gate to San Francisco or Sydney.

The vast space of the modern airport terminal means a little time spent just watching can be quite revealing. The fresh uniforms of airline pilots and cabin crews march with dogged determination to their aircraft, a disciplined purpose to their stride. Airline customer service agents smile serenely at their charges, always welcoming, always caring, always wanting to do more for you no matter which side of the bed they got out of that morning. From a purely personal perspective, one recent journey of my own, and my reason for it, was gratifyingly illustrated by the reaction from the gate agents just before boarding. Since the trip was work-related, I had copies of the magazines I contribute articles to with me and the agents were readers of them and they had read me – they knew who I was. But for most, despite the numbers, the terminal is still a place of anonymous interaction as thousands every hour pass through, each living their own moments; a small child scampers through his mother's legs in play as they wait, the businessman reads the financial pages, the holidaymaker checks again that sunscreen lotion has been packed. And then there is the flight…

The cabin crew smile their welcome and once everybody is seated on board the aircraft is pushed back and those with a window seat watch in morbid fascination or enthusiastic anticipation as the flaps extend for take-off, the safety announcements ignored… *'Heard it all before…read the safety cards already…yawn'*. Yet there are some (I am one) who still watch and listen then read again the safety instructions, no matter how many times they have been seen before. It's a ritual that I hope I never need to enact and unlikely as it is for most, it might one day prove its worth. As it could for everybody, no matter where the destination, be it Delhi or Dublin.

For the window-seated fan, the taxi to the runway is a joy-filled thrill, each bump and thump eagerly taken in as the aircraft threads its way along the yellow taxi line showing the pilot the way. Others may sit bored already; some may be gripping the armrests of their seat… *'Just get me there in one piece!'* The regular flier simply reads, pausing as they are pressed back in to their seat as the engines power up and speed the aircraft along the runway before rotation and the steep climb in to the sky. Then, unconcerned, continues to read.

Food and drinks are provided or purchased, depending on the airline. Low-fare carriers keep their fares low by not giving food away and the shorter the flight, the more costly it is to do so. But like the mall left behind, the profits are there if such things are sold. On a long flight as the hours pass, movies may be watched, music listened to. Today's flying experience has come a long way since the even longer time it took to get from Miami to Moscow and from Manchester to Montreal. Some just sleep since some things never change. The ability to sleep soundly during a long flight is priceless for those who can. Some can't but for those who have the money and fly in the right part of the aircraft, the sleeper seat is gold - just as it was in those far-off days when American Airlines introduced them on the DC3 in the 1930s before such seats gave way to the upright standard as the post-war era of mass travel dawned and then flowered brightly. The name of the game was to pack the passengers in, more seats mean more profits. Now, like the airport train, the sleeper seat has made a comeback if one has the extra cash or expense account to use one. Unless flying with a low-fare airline where sleeper seats are not to be found (one gets what one pays for) air travel, in some respects, has regressed to its future; more in-flight comfort means more passengers means full aircraft means more profits means staying in business.

Whatever the variety or vagaries of the flight itself, there is always the arrival. Whether from Abuja or Aberdeen, another ritual unfolds at the terminal; the aircraft stops and there is a rush to leave its confined space; the long haul flight has seen us, regardless of the class in which we have flown, tightly packed together, sharing our lives if we are socially-minded enough (and humankind is essentially a social animal). Even though we often value our quiet time, time on our own, we still

Flight

gravitate towards each other, sometimes because we have to but sometimes by choice. In the eight-and-a- half hours since leaving Dallas and arriving at London, we have no choice and most will at least acknowledge the presence of the other, a smile and a nod. No more than that but it makes the incarceration of the flight more palatable. For some the conversation had begun once on board or shortly after take off – suddenly nine hours has become nine minutes and the flight is over. Addresses are exchanged; a promise to get in touch made and we rush to leave.

There is then the hoped-for event of being reunited with one's bags, unless they have taken another flight to another place somewhere in the world. It does happen and although not common, neither are lost bags infrequent. For most people most of the time the bag stays with them and the wait at the baggage carousel leaves part of the mind on the beach or still at the place from where they departed. The frequent business trip might be a little different as thoughts turn to the office, the results of the journey still fresh and how to turn the meeting's proposal into reality. Whatever the purpose of the flight, with luggage and owner now together, the brief encounter at customs is, again for most, just that – brief.

For a few less so; Customs inspections can be revealing if there is something to hide, the illicit fruit, the undeclared high-value (and tax-payable) items, the often bungled attempt to secret somewhere those things one knows one should not have but wants anyway, such occasionally is the nature of a minority. The numbers who smuggle things are not great compared to those who do not but they are significant nonetheless.

But most travellers are not smugglers so pass through unmolested to Passport Control - business or pleasure? Hopefully both and again the time spent with an immigration officer is not long. For most people most of the time.

The arrivals hall is where the emotion of travel is unveiled. The banner welcoming home a student from their gap year, hugs from missed friends and relatives, the name on the hand-written sign, or even a professionally printed one, for Mr. X from Oslo by the driver of a limousine, waiting to whisk him swiftly to a tall tower in Tokyo. The sports squad, organisationally attired in eye-catching team travel wear, efficiently escorted to a luxury coach - or the lone traveller, unmet and heading in solitude towards the city-bound train.

Behind the flyer lies not only the memory of moments of their journey and from where they have come but also the aircraft that brought them to where they are now. On the other side of the terminal, it is now not an arrival but a departure, transforming itself from BA1793 to BA4820, or LH from FRA returning to FRA, UA7190 becoming UA7191. Ground Ops operate, the aircraft waits for its next group of passengers and it still takes seven hours and thirty minutes to fly from London to New York

For some, there are no memories for they have never been and never flown. The airport is something seen only on TV. Others find such a place only as means to an end, a place to pass through on their way from Sao Paulo to Stockholm and may be glad it is done and over with. Still more forget quickly and move on. Yet others think ahead to the next time, the time when they will return and never tiring of it, ask themselves, "Where shall we go tomorrow?", and again have their days and nights at the terminals and on the runways of the Airport.

∎

Leaving...Norwegian Boeing 737
(Tyler McDowell)

Channel Sunset
(Kevan James)

arriving....whatever the weather
(Kevan James)

Arrival
(Kevan James)

Printed in Great Britain
by Amazon